DEDICATED TO
The People of OLCC.
Together we have forged
a new identity.

Other Books by Robert L. Wise:

YOUR CHURNING PLACE
WHEN THERE IS NO MIRACLE

Contents

PREFACE

Once upon a time the air was clean and sex was dirty. Now the environment is polluted and all conceptions are immaculate. In that distant path, people vowed to stay together until death. Now they are concerned only to help each other get through the night.

Although this shift in values has happened in only a couple of decades, the changes represent an eon of social change. The result of such enormous readjustment is driving many people crazy.

In that ancient land of yesterday, we felt tension with those groups who acted "holier than thou." Now we are confronted with the new groupies whose intention is to be "weirder than thou." Beads and bell-bottoms have now been replaced by hot tubs and neighborhood nude bathing. Turquoise and Indian jewelry is worn by people who want to look Indian but wouldn't touch the lifestyle with a ten-foot pole. Truly a lot of people have lost their moorings somewhere along the way!

This brave new world we seem to have created has forced many of us to look elsewhere for better sources of stability. Yet many of the alternatives that have been suggested haven't been much better than the problems. We have been urged to "let it all hang out" as our salvation. However, that variety of honesty has often turned out to be just an unzipped mentality producing its own frenzied loose ends.

Against this background of indecision and misdirection, I started making my own quest for inner stability. To my surprise many of the answers were not novel nor innovative. Many of my discoveries have returned me to some of the bedrock ideas and conventions that have guided Western Civilization since its inception. I have been prompted to write because I find that too few people are in touch with these same sources of stability. Hopefully, these insights will help the reader recover a new sense of direction in these times that have surely gone awry.

I am indebted to a study group that served as a sounding board in helping me to frame the sources of some of the current national problems of instability. LeRoy Lake, Lou Clanahan, Dottie Chisholm, Lois Smith, and Dorothy Burshek all plowed through books, articles, and pamphlets in search for the cause of our current instability. Our discussions were the source of many insights and ideas.

Once again, Jane Cole Carter White and Fritz Ridenour provided invaluable assistance in readying the manuscript. My gracious secretary, Dorothy Waltz, has again gone the second mile in producing another manuscript. I am grateful for such talented friends.

—Robert L. Wise

Part I

When Everyone Else Has Gone Bananas

The Loss of Our Social Identity

A Crazy Little Conversation With John

We were discussing politics and the national scandals. As I argued with my friend, he kept using words and phrases like "misstatements" and "that answer is no longer operative."

"What do you mean?" I asked. "Every time I get you cornered you just dismiss any contradiction by changing the rules."

"Well," John said, "that's the way everything is today. Nothing is absolutely certain."

"Wait a minute!" I protested. "If every lie and misrepresentation can be erased by manipulating the English language, how can we ever find out the truth about anything?"

"The truth? The truth!" John responded rather indignantly. "Who knows what's absolutely true? Everything just depends on the individual's perspective."

I was astonished. "If there is no way to distinguish black, gray, or white, how can we tell whether we are in the night or day? How can anyone have any sense of direction?"

"Well," he said rather philosophically, "that's correct, I guess. But after all, life is just that way today."

And I thought, "That is utter madness!"

1

Henny Penny Was Right

I remember vividly the day I realized that Henny Penny was absolutely right.

Someone had recommended that I ought to see *Network*, a cinema satire on contemporary society. To my amazement I discovered that the hero was a national newscaster who had gone psychotic. Because Howard Beal suddenly began saying completely incredible, obscene statements on television, he became an overnight national hero. Though the man was mad, the network officials teamed him with a practicing witch named Sybil the Soothsayer. Together, Howard and Sybil captured a national audience of millions with their weekly TV specials.

Across America, multitudes tuned in to watch the witch and the psychotoc philosophize about life and the times. Finally, when the ratings dropped, in an attempt to recover their audience, the network arranged for the newscaster to be assassinated on television. *Network* suggested that everybody is *really* crazy these days. We are caught in a web of illusions and deceptions that completely masks reality. The inmates are running the institution!

As I left the theater it occurred to me that since I had paid four dollars to get in, maybe I was just as crazy as Howard Beal. I crossed the street to get a cup of coffee and to reflect on the meaning of the whole situation. As I stirred the coffee I watched a young family enter and sit down. Immediately they turned their five-year-old son loose on the restaurant. This pint-sized Howard Beal began running around the tables beating on people's arms and legs. The mother and father were completely oblivious as the miniature Godzilla terrorized everyone in sight.

Suddenly a current tune sprang from the jukebox. The song was "The Telephone Man," a confounding little ditty about a telephone installer who did a lot more to housewives than wire up their receivers. With the titillating song ringing in our ears, a child attacking total strangers, and the image of Howard and Sybil floating through my mind, I tried to find escape by looking out the window. My eyes focused on a blue sports car's bumper sticker, which read, "Henny Penny Was Right." Something deep inside me said, "Yeah, that's *absolutely* right!"

THE NEW CRAZIES

The sky has fallen in on millions of people around the world. We are living in a time of catastrophic change and social disintegration, and the effect leaves many of use extremely disoriented. Because of these chaotic conditions, instability is rampant.

I'm convinced that the net result is a new type of mental disorientation which can be called "the new crazies." And in fact, without publicly discussing it, we have developed our own social shorthand for expressing this instability. When we see someone who has been hit on the head by pieces of the falling sky we casually remark, "Well, he's gone bananas!" Or we may describe the problem by pointing out that the friend has "flipped out." Other current unscientific descriptions of the condition are "bongos," "nuts," "swonkers," "bonkers," or "spaced out."

Depending on the severity of the problem, the confused person may be labeled semi-bananas, half-bananas, or completely bananas. We immediately know what the situation is because we too have already felt that way three times the same day.

In previous decades, when someone went crazy he was taken off quietly to some secluded institution. Everyone could recognize that the poor person could no longer function, and needed special care. In addition, the doctors and the hospitals had various special labels with which to tag each mental disorder. So, while we were all saddened that someone we knew had broken down, we knew that craziness was the exception to the rule.

The new condition of craziness is completely different because, though hardly anyone is shipped off, most of the people we know are afflicted. All around us—crossing the streets, standing behind us in the supermarket, eating at our own table—are the people who have flipped out. Not only do we not institutionalize people "gone bananas," but we may make them into television stars, or national heroes, or elect them to public office.

Of course, we are relieved by the massive social acceptance of people who have gone crazy. We don't want to probe too deeply into what "going bananas" means, since we suspect we may actually be part of the problem. In the few moments of personal quiet reflection from which we flee, we know that life is becoming far more difficult than we can cope with. We become panicky that we are being bombarded by forces stronger than we can withstand. We yearn for real peace and quiet, and we hope that someone can help us glue the sky back together again.

So we need help in dealing with the many instabilities that are driving us crazy today. The answer of more "things" through materialism has obviously proven totally defective. A quick trip to the psychiatrist just hasn't filled the bill for millions of people. Though they end up with scientific labels for their problems, many of the people are just as bananas as before. People have tried diets, health foods, and personal-encounter movements as their salvation. Still the sky keeps falling.

These pages are written to help you find some specific directions for dealing with the disorienting forces attacking our lives. By sifting through the pressures of modern living, some key discoveries can be found that will help put the sky back in place.

GETTING IT FROM ALL SIDES

These pressures that cause the modern crazies are coming at us from at least two directions. First, something destructive is happening to us *internally*. We are being overwhelmed by the conflicts within us. Society's radical changes are compounding our personal emotional tensions. Too often the result can prevent us from remembering who we really are and where we came from. We feel cut loose from any real roots, but we're not really sure where we're going!

One broad diagnosis for this confusion might be a "contemporary identity crisis." The effect is a sensation of disorientation and a feeling of being a little crazy much of the time. In Part II we'll delve further into these reasons for making us flip out, and we'll discover how we can recover our personal identity.

However, in the next three chapters we will explore the forces that are bombarding us *externally*. We are being hit from all sides with conflicts that can turn our lives into a scenario from *Network*. All of us need help in combating the effects that social confusion has on us personally.

We are living in a time of social disorientation and disintegration. The instabilities in society creep into our thought processes. When institutions no longer function and social values are crumbling, uncertainty creeps down inside us. Once we lose our confidence in the decisions of our national leaders, we also tend to feel a personal lack of confidence in the other road signs that direct our individual decisions. The result has a debilitating effect, and we feel that everything and everyone is going nuts!

How did we get into this mess? Well, this phenomenon didn't happen overnight. We've been struggling with the impact of social disillusionment for some time now. In the sixties, Joan Didion explored the hippie movement and sought answers for this radical rejection of parents, church, and society. In *Slouching Towards Bethlehem,* she came to these conclusions:

> *We were seeing the desperate attempt of a handful of theoretically unequipped children to create a community in a social vacuum. Once we had seen these children, we could no longer overlook the vacuum, no longer pretend that the society's atomization could be reversed. This was not a traditional generational rebellion. At some point between 1945 and 1967 we had somehow neglected to tell these children the rules of the game we happened to be playing. Maybe we had stopped believing in the rules ourselves, maybe we were having a failure of nerve about the game.*[1]

This loss of faith in the rules and this disillusionment about social interaction has produced not only a rebellion of young people but also a crippling emotional paralysis that has left millions feeling that the world no longer makes sense. And the result? Well, here are a couple of examples from my counseling practice.

As the middle-aged lady sat across from my desk, she dabbed at her eyes with a tissue. In a faltering voice she said, "At 45 my husband had reached every goal he set for himself. We have a comfortable home and make more money than I ever dreamed possible. Actually our kids are great and have given us no problems to speak of."

Then her voice trailed off almost into a whisper. She sighed deeply and continued. "But last night John came home and told me that life makes no sense at all.

Nothing makes him happy or satisfied. So he is leaving me for his secretary and says he hopes to find a new start in life."

Still another woman shared with me her story of leaving a husband. She told me how he was really quite a good man. He came home every night, worked in the yard, and was a fine father. Yet life had lost its magic for her.

"I read the women's liberation books and decided there was something golden out there I was missing." In a matter-of-fact tone she continued, "So one day I just said goodbye and set out for something called a career. It almost killed my husband."

Then her voice increased in intensity. "Now I'm miserable and don't have any idea of what's right or wrong, or what direction my life needs to take."

Later both women said, "Sometimes I just feel like I'm going crazy." Indeed! The pressure was coming on all sides, and they felt miserable!

THE LOST NEW WORLD

Let's examine some of the reasons why today's pressures are bearing down with such overwhelming force. Clarifying some of the sources of the confusion will help us push the pieces back up into the sky. Surprising as it might seem, "newness" is a major part of the problem.

We are living in a completely new world! Our vocabulary is filled with words and phrases that did not exist before 1950. Consider words like lifestyle, corporate man, interpersonal relationships, plastics, miracle drugs, etc. In spite of all their familiarity, these are brand-new additions to our everyday conversation. Moreover, consider our contemporary slang.

Recently I had such a contemporary conversation with a young man who is a fine artist. "I really like this watercolor you've done," I said,

"Yeah, far out, isn't it!" He said enthusiastically. "I really get off on watercolor!"

I responded, "The light reflections in your picture really are a trip."

"I can groove on color," he said. "The more I get into illuminosity the heavier it gets. Light and color really blow my mind."

Later I reflected to myself, "No wonder no one communicates anymore! I'm not even sure what we said to each other."

We are being bombarded by new knowledge at a rate that is impossible to synthesize.

Words, slang, new ideas roll in from every side. It is nearly impossible to keep up with the specialized conversation of your children, your working spouse, and your friends.

In *Future Shock* Alvin Toffler describes how this influx of change can leave us short-circuited and unable to respond. Toffler calls the feeling "shock." The world of computers didn't exist before 1960, but now our lives are run by these machines. With hundreds of other examples Toffler shocks you as you simply read his book.

Drug usage and smoking "grass" were unthinkable just 20 years ago. Yet today professional people are users just as often as adolescents. Of course the sexual revolution confronts us with a national shift in moral values. Change has become the norm of the day.

All this newness has left us without familiar guides to direct our thinking and acting. We find ourselves unsure and with a loss of nerve about what to do next. The new age has not given us the direction we needed. An abundance of data has been dumped on us without instructions on how to proceed. We have entered into a new era that has lost its way!

WARNING SIGNS

The statistical results of our confusion are staggering. By applying national norms to my own community of Oklahoma City, I discovered some alarming predictions. In any community of 600,000 people, mental health statistics predict that we can expect the following consequences.[2] Out of every 12,000 children born annually, 2400 will require psychiatric care to function. During their lifetimes over a thousand of those born will be confined to a mental hospital.

Recent statistics from New York City suggest that there will be more abortions in any given year than live births! So potentially some 12,000 unborn babies will have had their lives terminated.

Forty percent of the surviving babies will someday apply for the military but will be rejected. One-third of these rejectees will be set aside because of mental and emotional problems.

In this community of 600,000 people there will be 600 attempted suicides, and 80 of them will succeed. Each year 3200 people will require institutional confinement and major psychiatric treatment in order to function.

Consideration of these statistics leads to perplexing conclusions. While newness has brought more affluence, instability continues to increase. Our seemingly expanded knowledge and growing collection of facts has brought with it an increased inability to function.

Four countries at the top of the highest per-capita income in the world are Sweden, the United States, Switzerland, and Denmark. Correspondingly they also have the highest rate of suicide, homicide, and alcoholism![3]

Something has slipped badly in our "brave new world"!

The looting that resulted from the 1977 blackout in New York City makes this verdict inescapable. Over 3700 people went on a rampage through the stores of the darkened areas. After these New Yorkers were arrested and booked, these alarming facts came to light.

Nearly half of the looters were regularly employed. About 40 percent of those arrested were enrolled in some government antipoverty program! Fewer than 10 percent were on welfare. Actually the average personal income of this group was approximately the same as the national average of the general population.[4]

This swarm of human locusts did not devour those stores out of hunger or economic deprivation. The looters simply did not have the internal moral values to keep them from "going crazy." "Newness" had removed the traditional value systems and left nothing in its place.

The truth is that most of us spend our leisure time trying to escape the onslaught of newness and pressure that pours in on us during the workday. We sense a need to get away from it all. In *The Sane Society*, Eric Fromm suggests that if movies, television, sports events, and newspapers were cut off for four weeks, millions would be gripped by acute anxiety. As a psychiatrist, he predicts that if all the avenues of personal escape were blocked, thousands of people would have nervous breakdowns.[5] Newness and change are simply overwhelming us.

SKEPTICAL FAITH

Another significant factor in our disorientation is our own disillusionment.

Loss of confidence in social structures, systems, leaders, and relationships undermines individual self-confidence. We need to be able to believe in the external factors that shape our lives in order to be in a position to feel secure about our personal decisions. Today our national doubts are having a serious personal effect.

For the past year I have been running a personal survey through the groups to whom I speak. In all parts of the country I have asked individuals to share with me their candid opinions about American people. They are asked to answer the question, "What do you think motivates the average American citizen?" When the results were tabulated I was amazed! The following three responses ranked one, two, and three with a majority of those polled.

First, the majority of people answered that selfishness is the prime factor in personal decisions. Many said that their friends are "deceitful" or "rip-off artists." Later, in discussing their answers with the total group, they often lashed out at the massive corporations, such as oil companies and auto manufacturers. Many of these people believe that they are being consistently lied to and cheated at every turn.

The second-most-suggested answer was that everyone is motivated by a lust for power. Many times the groups answered that people are greedy and will attempt to gain all possible control over others. Usually the conversation drifted to examples such as Richard Nixon or the Korean influence-buying scandal. People were inclined to believe that everyone should be eyed with suspicion. If the President of the United States is a proven liar, then who knows about anybody else? So the line of reasoning goes.

A third consistent response was that people are manipulators. The group felt that many people are manipulators interested only in personal gain. Recently, a lady reminded one group of the discovery that a series of Oldsmobiles had been equipped with Chevrolet engines, and that customers had been deceived about this switch. "See," she said, "and lots of people I know are just as crafty!"

Whether these assertions are true, or even fair, isn't the issue. The point is that millions of people think and feel they must be constantly on guard. They are disillusioned, and their faith in others has failed.

When we think everyone is out to get us, we can become defensive in ways that affect our mental health. The clinical diagnosis for such a condition is paranoia, and the contemporary expression is "Bananas."

But you're not only interested in getting insight into what's going on—you want some answers! In addition to analyzing these sources of stress, you are looking for solutions to problems of everyday living. Therefore, the last half of each chapter will suggest alternatives and new approaches for contending with our unstable world. So let's start on a new direction.

WE NEED A CHANGE!

We need a new orientation! A radical break has to be made from the pressures that are bearing down upon us. Because there is little that can be done to change our social environment, the change has to happen *inside* us.

It is possible to develop a new perspective on your ideas, your dreams, and your self-understanding that will bring a real stability into your life. When you discover a new sense of what your life can mean, the disconcerting effects of change can be broken.

For example, just discovering a new perspective on your relationship to society could make a difference. For many people, finding a real and lasting meaning for their life would be tremendously settling. Orientation is very much a matter of the right facts.

What you believe is crucial because all of us live, think, act, trust, and plan around assumptions which can't be proven. We all must live by faith of some kind of variety. The real question is whether our faith assumptions are true and if they work for us.

We have already seen how lots of crazies result from our current disillusionments. In addition, we surveyed the results of change when people are cut loose from the moorings that once guided them. Lost faith means lost direction.

Movies like *Network* also tell us something more: that trusting in the wrong ideas, values, or dreams will produce painful despair. Defective faith, like bad apples, will corrupt whatever else it touches. So getting oriented demands that what we believe must be valid!

This principle of orientation is crucial and basic to personal stability. Here's an example of why we must be on target. You would assume that people who attend churches should be in touch with what makes for a correct faith. Yet there are many, many church people who are experiencing the crazies. Why?

The truth is that often American church people are far more products of their culture than they are of their faith. Quite often their social behavior and personal convictions are in complete contradiction to what they profess on Sunday. Therefore, because they are actually shaped by the society, when the culture shakes they feel the vibrations in the pits of their stomachs.

Regardless of what we say we believe in, our personal orientation hinges on our real faith assumptions. If we are feeling bananas, then we can know that something needs to be worked on in the realm of our convictions.

Not only beauty, but also meaning, is in the eye of the beholder. While you may feel that the world out there is tearing you apart, the truth is that the stress is basically in your head. Much of the time the tension lies in how you are viewing the flow of events.

What's happening in the current turmoil of change is not as important as what we believe about it and how we interpret the meaning of our experience. If we have the ability to reinterpret our conflicts in a new light, we can transform their meaning. Actually, a valid faith can put the pieces of the sky back together.

WHAT SHOULD WE BELIEVE?

Thus far we have seen that the radical deluge of the "new" hasn't really helped us acquire a stable perspective. Perhaps what we need is something "old" for a change.

Rather than just watching society fly past and being bewildered, we need a proven direction from a faith that can turn tension into trust. And I've found a clue to stability through studying the lives of Christian people who have lived in past generations. Living with radical change was nothing new to that unbroken chain of believers who, through the centuries, have been called the church. In fact, some of their most heroic stories occurred during the worst of times.

What they believed helped them to see the world differently from their contemporaries. The Roman world differently disappeared into the dark ages. Through faith, Augustine saw a whole new plan for the society which was to follow. As the medieval world melted into the Renaissance, men like Luther and Calvin found faith assumptions that guided the new age forward. Individuals like Galileo, Pascal, Sir Thomas More, Tyndale, Thomas Aquinas, and an army of other Christians had critical minds and personal stability because of their faith.

These stable people of vision had an unusual common denominator that is rare today. Their perspective on the times was marked by an unusual detachment from the flow of events. They were able to shake free the bondage to the "old" and the prejudices that held their contemporaries. They had the stability not to be frightened by change, and they could give leadership to the new day dawning.

What is this extraordinary attribute? I stumbled across the answer in reading the stories of some very ancient men of faith who also had endured times of catastrophic change and upheaval. Interestingly enough, this record is found in a letter written to the Jewish people to help them make the transition during that monumental shift in history following the birth of Jesus Christ.

The eleventh chapter of the Book of Hebrews describes how the ancient men of God remained stable. In citing examples like Abraham, Moses, David, and others, the author repeatedly refers to the role their faith played in their decisions. A paragraph that begins in verse 13 uncovers the answer we are seeking.

> . . . *having acknowledged that they were strangers and exiles on the earth. For people who speak thus make it clear that they are seeking a homeland. If they had been thinking of that land from which they had gone out, they would have had opportunity to return. But as it is, they desire a better country, that*

> *is, a heavenly one. Therefore God is not asham-*
> *ed to be called their God, for He has prepared*
> *for them a city.*

They had a pilgrim mentality! We must discover how such a mind operates.

In a literary sense, a pilgrim is someone who sees life as a journey. I am not thinking of the sixteenth-century founding fathers with their black hats and silver-buckle shoes. Rather, this variety of pilgrim has a perception of life as an adventure. They are always traveling toward and finding deeper and more signifi-cant meaning in their existence.

THE SOJOURNERS' SECRET

While deeply concerned with their own societies and attempting to make everyday life better, each of these people's vision was focused on a higher horizon line. These dynamic persons of faith loved life and savored the joy of living. Yet they moved in a dimension which lifted them above and beyond the immediate moment. Their pilgrim mentality was the critical detachment from their contemporary problems that put these everyday concerns into perspective.

A pilgrim mentality is not only concerned with now, but is also moving toward the future. With such a perspective one not only listens to his or her contem-poraries, but also measures their opinions by what God has clarified through the centuries. Ultimately, a pilgrim mentality realizes that you *don't* live just once. Feeling the responsibility of eternity, the pilgrim orien-tation is not captured by time and the tyranny of the urgent.

The sojourner's secret can help us clarify our relation-ship to culture and change. If we see ourselves as "strangers and exiles on earth" we will not believe that any of our social situations are final. Rather than being molded by the society, we can become products of our faith. This detachment will keep us from being deceived by secondary matters and from missing what really counts.

We will not make the mistake of making the world around us ultimate. Such a subtle distinction is extraordinarily important, and those who haven't known the difference have paid a great price for their lack of perception. World War Two left us with tragic and almost unspeakable examples of what can happen when the things of the culture are too important.

The specter of millions of Jews being slaughtered by the Nazis continues to haunt Western civilization. As sociologists have pondered how such a massacre could be possible, they have noted a strange contradiction. As early as 1935 (or even earlier) many people saw the exterminations coming. While some of the Jewish population read the signs of the times and left, the majority remained. In many instances they clearly closed their eyes to the inevitable. Why?

Many social scientists feel the answer is clear. The lingering Jewish population were so tied to their homes, accumulations, things, and cultural attachments that they closed their eyes to what was happening. Though Abraham was their father, they had ceased to be "strangers and exiles." Setting into the culture cost them their lives.

OUR WORLD OF POSSESSIONS

In a similar way, whether Christian or non-Christian, many moderns are utterly locked into our world of possessions. When the society of dishwashers, automobiles, and microwave ovens doesn't work, we fall apart too.

While our enemies are not as easily identified as were the Nazis, they are just as real. The forces of materialism, consumerism, and secularism are powerful marching through our lives, stripping away the meaning and purpose that is essential for a sense of well-being. Though we don't end up in concentration camps, many of us are equally victimized by the despair and futility we feel in our everyday experience.

In contrast, Hebrews describes the Christian sojourner as being motivated by the quest for a heavenly homeland. The pilgrim, who is always concerned with the good of his place in history, discovers life to be very full as he pushes for something much larger than just what he finds around himself. On the other hand, the people who only aim at this world can't keep even that.

Perhaps this might suggest a whole new orientation to you. I have found that such a faith perspective really does work. In fact, I have seen these insights bring powerful new hope to distressed people.

Remember the story of the woman whose 45-year-old husband ran off with the secretary? In the beginning she felt as though she would actually go crazy. Overwhelming depression swept over her life. Even after she made some initial adjustments to her loss, nagging sensations of having flipped out kept haunting her.

The real turning point came the afternoon she accepted a pilgrim mentality. In the midst of a counselling session she blurted out, "Wait a minute, Robert! That man isn't the whole story of my life! Yes, God does have much more for me. Though I have been hurt, I believe that there will be new chapters ahead if I let Him help me write them."

That afternoon she became a pilgrim. Though she had hoped to settle into some small niche somewhere, God took her tragedy and turned her life into a marvelous new adventure. Though all of her problems did not vanish, faith's direction and confidence gave her life enduring stability.

And the woman who left her husband? Unfortunately, time had taken its own toll, and their relationship could not be restored. However, as she took on the pilgrim identity her craziness began to disappear. Today, with a new husband and career, living has great purposes for her.

Why? Because she measures everything and makes all her decisions by the highest possible orientation to life. As a sojourner she truly is going somewhere.

HOW ABOUT YOU?

Do you need this revolution? Is there a possibility that a pilgrim mentality could keep the sky from constantly falling down around you? The sojourner spirit might be just what you've been needing to get circumstances back into perspective.

Here's a specific way to find out: check yourself out to discover where you really live. I don't mean to look up your street address. In this day and time, we are so mobile that our apartments, condominiums, and houses hardly reflect where we actually reside.

Rather, I'm talking about the place where your soul and spirit live. You reside in the place of your fantasies and hopes. The mental compartments where you make your plans, enjoy your dreams, mull over your worries, and experience your deepest satisfactions are your true living place.

Quietly get in touch with this place, because it is where you panic as well.

Ask yourself three questions:

1. What dreams motivate my life?
2. What is the basis for my sense of security?
3. What do I require to be truly happy?

Perhaps you might want to write this down and elaborate what each answer means. You will be defining your hopes and values; your sources of personal satisfaction will also surface.

After you've achieved some clarification, start asking yourself about how permanent and enduring these answers are. Carefully analyze the composition of your hopes and dreams. Can they really last and will they carry you through rocky times of possible discouragement and disillusionment? Is it possible that you are tied to goals that will perish and crumble?

If so, you've found an important insight into why you find yourself "going bananas." You have discovered the source of some of the shakiness in your life.

In the pages ahead we will explore further how to develop a sojourner orientation that will undergird you with vitality and endurance for facing every tension that confronts you. We can do this with complete confidence, because all pilgrims have a tremendous promise. Through Jesus Christ, God promised to liberate us from fear, and pledges to give us a sound mind (2 Timothy 1:7).

But we must begin by being ruthlessly honest with ourselves. Our superficiality and artificiality get us into trouble. The writer of Hebrews has given us the better directions. If we will let go of the deceptions by which we live, God is anxious to replace the transitory with the permanent. An orientation of faith will give us the same citizenship and homeland that the stable saints of the past enjoyed. You can start living in that heavenly city right now. And in God's city the sky doesn't fall!

1. Joan Didion, *Slouching Towards Bethlehem* (New York: Dell Publishing Co., 1968).
2. Lealon E. Martin, *Mental Health/Mental Illness* (New York: McGraw Hill, 1970), Chapter VI.
3. Eric Fromm, *The Sane Society*, (Rinehart & Co., 1955), Chapter 1.
4. *The Daily Oklahoman*, August 16, 1977.
5. Fromm, *The Sane Society*.

2

"Now" Isn't Enough!

We really ought to finish the Henny Penny story. You'll remember that the chicken frantically ran across the countryside, sounding the alarm that the sky was falling in. Quickly she collected a menagerie of barnyard friends, who hysterically added their emotions and fears to the cry that the world was coming to an end. Finally the wily and perceptive wolf decided that he would cash in on the act.

With all gracious hospitality, the wolf offered shelter to the irrational caravan. Opening the door to his cave, he ushered them in with the assurance that they could find underground protection from the imminent disaster. After the door was shut and bolted, he promptly sat down to dinner—composed of chicken, duck, and other tender morsels from the barnyard!

THE MORAL OF THE STORY

An important moral lurks here in the shadows. The emotions of people who have gone a little crazy tend to get them gobbled up as they run loose in the world.

Of course, that's what you and I are experiencing every day. The wolf may come in a great many forms and disguises, but the effect is the same. We feel like modern society is eating us alive! No, most of us are not pilgrims and sojourners moving with a vision that penetrates through the modern confusion surrounding us. We are caught up in the chaos!

While living in Southern California I experienced my first earthquake. The physical sensations of a tremor are like the internal effects of the modern crazies. You feel as if nothing has any stability or balance.

An earthquake shakes everything that you had always believed was permanent. Not only do the furniture and windows seem to be in motion, but the floor and the ground are shifting beneath your feet. With every point of reference quivering, the experience is terrifying. There is nothing left to cling to, and you find yourself at the mercy of impersonal and indifferent forces that are bringing your world down around your ankles. All perspective is lost as your survival becomes everything! You are swallowed up in the "now" moment.

Social earthquakes are no less devastating. Their sensation makes it doubly difficult to hang onto the pilgrim mentality we so desperately need. Contemporary life has forced everything into the present tense, but stability demands foundations that surround us and extend ahead into the future. Without spiritual perceptiveness the wolf has got us! "Now" simply isn't enough perspective to bring stability to our lives.

Life that is completely absorbed by the present moment tends to become "bonkers." Bonkers is a synonym for "losing your marbles." These and the many other phrases are the comic ways we talk about the emotional and mental disorientation left by the social earthquakes. In the first chapter I discussed these crazies in a rather casual vein.

Actually, my intention is far broader than that. While we haven't developed textbook categories for this problem of "bananas," I am convinced that American society is gripped by a new emotional condition that is very urgent.

Previously we had usually thought of people as being basically either sane or crazy. Everyone seemed to be essentially either rational or irrational. The deranged people needed specific treatment and emotional care. In addition, we had definite labels that told us what their problems were. Our definitions for schizophrenia, paranoia, manic depressive, etc., gave us security about ourselves. Since we weren't in any of those boxes, we could relax and know that we were stable.

But something different has now developed—a middle ground has evolved. It is as if we now have a foot in each of these worlds! Sometimes we seem stable and at other times we know we are very unstable. While we may go on functioning in an acceptable social manner, our thinking and feeling is distorted. Too often we're not sure on which side of the line we're actually standing.

The old explanations for instability come through cause-and-effect results from previous developmental experiences. Usually in early childhood, painful interpretations of life events had deeply scarred the person. The key word for self-understanding was *psychology*.

This new condition has developed from other sources. We find that we are unable to interpret the meaning of our present experiences. Life is out-of-focus because we aren't able to make adequate sense of what's happening to us and where we're going. So today's key word is *philosophy*. The problems do not arise only from our emotions but are also pouring in from the social pressures around us. We just can't get an adequate interpretation of what our life means.

PAYING FOR PRAYING?

Let me give you an example of a life totally poured into the now moment but lived without any meaning. Recently a young woman came to see me. She wanted to pay me to pray for her. I was staggered! I assured her that I prayed for people and would pray with her, but that money had nothing to do with my concern.

"Well," Mary said, "everything else that counts is a matter of money. So I thought this kind of help would require a check."

"Heavens, no! Surely you don't feel that concern and caring can be bought!" I tried to assure her that something much deeper was involved in why we tried to help people.

And from there she unfolded an amazing story. Mary had inherited a rather large estate and had money to burn. But she had not been able to find anyone who loved her just for herself. Mary had gone from man to man. Every relationship ended in emptiness and loneliness.

Finally Mary had begun to live only with men who "kept" her. Though she was wealthy, getting something monetary out of her sexual relationships gave her some sense of value when the affair was over. Love and warmth was gone, but the fur coats and cars remained.

She wanted me to pray for her because she felt she was losing her mind. Everything had lost its meaning, and the void was marked only by persistent depression. Mary went right on about the business of buying and selling, having casual liaisons, and keeping a full social calendar. But philosophically and emotionally she was dead. The wolf was at her door morning and night. Far from being a pilgrim, the "now" moment had completely overtaken her.

Such experiences demand that we explore further what contributes to the development of this new earthquake—shaken mentality. And one very significant ingredient is the current total preoccupation of our culture with life, and the conviction that "you only go around once."

WHEN LIFE BECOMES A BLUR

Daily we are bombarded by the suggestion that we only have the next instant in which to live our lives. If we don't "do it now," the golden nectar of living will run through our fingers and be forever lost. So we have become preoccupied with living only for this moment.

However, the result has not been fulfilling. In fact, our experience of life and time has become so distorted that our balance is affected. Some of the crazies we have are the product of the twentieth-century way of bending and twisting the flow of time.

Today we often experience time as being "out-of-sync." The usual synchronization between the flow of events out of the past through this moment and on into the future has been interrupted and chopped apart. Because we seem to be cut loose from past history and without significant relationship to the future, life feels out of kilter.

Generally we don't stop at a given instant and reflect on what has happened to us. In fact, we may have little awareness at all of what is going on. Rather, we sense that the meaning of life just doesn't stretch past the day we were born. The result is that we don't feel anchored to anything permanent. And since the future doesn't seem to have any great significance, we lack the feeling that we are really going anywhere.

So life becomes a blur. We thought each of those individual "gusto" moments was what it was all about. Yet as we look back over our shoulder, those experiences smear together without any particular significance or great worth. Along with Mary and a multitude of "now-generation" people we discover that our life seems adrift in a liquid sea of indecision and insignificance. We find ourselves too bewildered to explain why the now hasn't been enough.

THE THREE INGREDIENTS

There are at least three basic ingredients in our distorted impression of time. Each of these elements is important because of the subtle pressure it places on us. In addition, any one of these factors can cause us to feel slightly bananas.

First, we are under a constant bombardment of change. Events happen with such swiftness and come from so many directions that we are unable to digest their meaning. Constant revision and change in the social rules leaves us like shell-shocked soldiers whose responses are no longer appropriate. As time is accelerated we are left with even more emotional dizziness. Alvin Toffler's *Future Shock* describes this effect in great detail.

What would happen if the food service in a cafeteria line were suddenly speeded up? Normally you have ample time to reflect on each choice. At a pleasant pace you select a balanced meal that is pleasing to your taste. As you come to the end of the line you feel satisfied and in a good mood to enjoy the meal.

But suddenly the line starts moving faster and faster. The waitresses begin shoving food from behind the counter.

"Here, take this! Try this one! Take two! Quickly, faster, others are waiting!" And as they shout at you they are forcing food into your hands.

Jello slides into mashed potatoes, and gravy is running over into the lettuce salad. When you come to the end of the line you feel frantic and angry. Your choices are lost and you end up with whatever falls on your plate. You conclude that the cafeteria has gone mad.

When you are the object of such an emotional bombardment of constant change, you are the one who seems to have gone bonkers. Aspirin brings only temporary relief, for the cycle starts all over as soon as you leave for work each day.

Second, we are staggered by the intensity of today's experiences. Events fall upon us with a thunderclap that rattles our whole nervous system. From our first waking moment until sleep comes, we are caught in a high-pressure barrage of sights, sounds, and vibrations that keep us on constant edge. The result is that we lose our quiet, reflective center that is vital to a sense of well-being.

For example, do you remember the last time you drove down a major boulevard in any city? Recall how you were constantly attacked by flashing neon signs, whirling ornaments, swerving cars, and flying banners. Almost every inch of sidewalk made a new demand on your vision. Hot dog stands, furniture stores, pizza parlors, car lots, etc. were crying out for you to stop and look. Soon you began to tune everything out. To have any concentration left demanded that you tune out the whole scene. So you ended up not really seeing any of it. There were simply too many stimuli to be digested.

In the same way, the intensity of events and emotional experiences causes us to develop our own internal bewilderment. We are asked to make one major decision after another. At the same time we have constant new bits of data poured in upon us. Soon we lose the emotional energy needed to fully digest what is happening to us. We're no longer sure of the appropriate response.

Slowly but surely we lose touch with the quiet, creative center of our lives. We can no longer hollow out a retreat place within ourselves. As we get pushed out of touch with ourselves, we can't be sure what we really want or need. In the end, time is an ever greater enemy that continually pushes us harder and faster to reach we know not what!

Third, we have lost synchronization because so often the now moment doesn't have significant meaning. Whenever life seems distorted or twisted we feel ourselves lost in a maze of pointless turns and twists. The loss of meaning is always experienced as a loss of direction.

Here's an example of how our cycle of living has been severely distorted by modern advertising. Formerly, you grew up, developed maturity, and moved into old age with direction and decision. Now the ad tells us that aging is unacceptable. Getting old means losing vitality and virility. As people frantically try to hang onto fleeing youth, their own life cycle seems to actually work against them. So an unavoidable maturation process has no point to it.

Moreover, everyday life seems to be so broken and unpredictable that needed patterns don't emerge to help us feel stable. With over 50 percent of the nation's marriages ending in divorce, the family structure no longer promises to give us a reason for our work and dreams. Too often, charting our life's course and flow of events produces a seismograph-like chart of continuing highs and lows. And these ups and downs just don't seem to be going anywhere. Without meaning, each day ends up being only another pointless part of the blur going past us with increasing speed.

The sum total of this loss of sync leaves us wavering unsteadily between feeling rational and feeling emotionally disturbed. If all three of these factors converge on us at the same time, we may indeed find ourselves so overwhelmed and distressed that we may actually go a little crazy if we don't find some immediate relief!

LIFE IN THE NOW

Some relief and definite help *is* on the way! Getting a handle on what has happened to us will begin to lift us above the maze of confusion we feel. We need to analyze and diagnose how and why we are being eaten alive.

Basically, too much weight has been placed on the "now" moment. The contemporary preoccupation with "live now" has cut us loose from moorings that are essential for our emotional well-being. The past has been declared to be insignificant and the future unobtainable. So all the importance of history has been drained from our perspective, and any orientation that the future might give has been draped in a cloak of irrelevance. Everything of value has been poured into the present moment. The problem is that living only for today can't carry the emotional load of our existence.

Subtly and unconsciously, the surrounding culture has sold us a bill of goods. The message is slipped to us at the corner movie theater and in most of the serious drama we watch on television. Yet we are being misled.

The most pervasive art form of our times is the cinema. Watch the presuppositions that operate in the script and you'll get the message that the celluloid artists are ending us. Most serious movies today are hammering out a similar philosophical statement about the now moment. You can almost choose at random and hear their point.

"Midnight Cowbody," "The Day of the Locust," "Looking for Mr. Goodbar," etc. have no similarity in plot, but they each have the same distinct message about life: there is no meaning to yesterday and no significance for the future. All you're going to get is what you can grab right now.

That philosophical twist has developed a new and strange type of hero. Today's central figure of the cinema is not really a hero but an antihero. The good guy is the character who is slightly better than the rest of the bad guys. "The Godfather" left you rooting for the Coreleones to kill the other Mafia figures, who were just a bit more base. Morality is no longer the issue. The hero is the one who can grab the most and survive, regardless of the cost.

Today the traditional loser has become the winner. Since there is really no meaning to life, the actor can supply purpose only by acting on his impulses. James Bond is a great hero because he can kill so indiscriminately and with so little emotional involvement. Grabbing the sex, the power, the money, etc. gives his life the appearance of excitement and fullness. We like to fantasize ourselves as Agent 007, but for some reason, when we attempt his lifestyle it never seems to work out that way for us.

These contemporary film messages are simple. Since you only have this illusive moment, get everything you can NOW. Unless you fill your living with sensuous and exciting experiences, there will be nothing left but emptiness.

This life philosophy is selling lots of tickets at the box office, it isn't bringing much happiness on the home front. The truth is that this message is a major factor in why life is making so little sense for so many people.

An abiding sense of well-being can be found only as we get things back into a larger and more significant perspective. We must place today in a framework that has a past and looks toward a future.

Our difficulty in doing exactly that is no accident. Our society didn't just happen to slip into this preoccupation with today. Actually we have been moving in this direction for well over 30 years. However, recently the effect has become so widespread that the problem can be clearly diagnosed as a total cultural condition. Here is how the situation developed.

THE NEW IDEA

In the late forties the atomic bomb wasn't the only explosion that rocked America. A new philosophical idea began to explode in the American scene, and its power sent shock waves far into the future. The real impact of the blast and the fiery flash became more evident in the sixties. Pieces of everyday life were scattered around the terrain as traditional values and institutions crumpled and sagged under the heat. In the late seventies the pieces began to settle again.

That philosophy is called *existentialism*. Though it has come with many inflections and shades of interpretations, we can clearly describe the essential effect that this school of thought has had on our perception of meaning. <u>The existentialist believes that life has no purpose except what an individual chooses to give it.</u> Though this is an oversimplification, this ideology teaches that there are no absolutes. Everything is simply relative. So the past and future do not have any inherent meaning!

The existentialist believes that the way to find any point in life lies in "happening" onto some extraordinary "experience" that you alone decide can give ultimate direction to your being around. That experience could be found in stealing, helping, being promiscuous, being constructive, being destructive, etc. It's all up to you.

While you might not recognize the name "existentialism," this way of thinking is the main system of thought behind our current preoccupation with the contemporary.

Make no mistake—I am not describing an interesting debate about existence that might go on in the philosophy department of some university. The whole matter certainly began there, but currently these conclusions have filtered beyond novels and textbooks into our national bloodstream. Without realizing the difference, we have grown to accept these interpretations of life as being completely true. Being totally preoccupied with today has become as natural as eating breakfast every morning.

TAMING TIME

Do you have the picture? When life becomes a blur we are going to feel smeared! Our contemporary existentialists preoccupations and conclusions are doing us in. "Now" not only isn't enough—it has become too much!

We simply have to get our experience of time back into a better focus. Once again, our personal orientation and perspective is crucial to our sense of sanity. There just has to be a better balance than the one we find in the movies and in popular opinion.

I have discovered that a pilgrim mentality has additional insights that can help us get through our present muddle. The Christian sojourner can sort out the transient from the permanent and knows other secrets about the meaning of time. By exploring these discoveries I have found a definite release from the frantic urgency that seems ready to invade my soul each waking moment.

The sojourner is something like a time traveler. In contrast to people who can't get beyond today, he is living with a definite sense of time flow that is strongly linked to the past and yet is lived in anticipation of the future. Events and decisions are weighed on a balance scale. "Now" is the fulcrum point, but the past and future are equal sides of the scales. The simple act of measuring and balancing the worth of a given moment can restore a great deal of emotional stability.

These modern pilgrim time travelers get their special sense of time by acquiring a biblical perspective on history. The Bible itself has a unique quality. If not the oldest, certainly it is one of the most ancient books we have. Its history is ancient and prescientific, but every new generation is gripped again and again by its message. While concerned with events in past time, the Bible seems to be timeless. This special quality filters into the emotions and thoughts of the sojourner. Personal stability just naturally follows.

DIGGING OUT THE STORY

In order to tame time we need to dig out the inside story. How does the Bible view history? What difference is there between a pilgrim view and the existentialist ideas? How can a biblical perspective restore balance?

First, the Bible says that history is very important. Scripture begins not *outside* history but as a prelude to it. Then the narrative moves quickly to affirm that all human events are important. They are to be remembered and discussed. The past is always important and of great significance. Yesterday is never to be treated as being inconsequential. The light of the past is crucial to having a clear vision of what is happening today.

Second, the Bible has a particular reason for having such a strong interest in the past. While history is empty and without any absolute meaning to the existentialist, the pilgrim believes that the past is crammed full of significance. In the very flow of human events, God reveals Himself. Therefore the past is filled with clues about our own meaning and destiny.

The Bible has collected those crucial moments when God moved to impart a special meaning to our existence. In biblical history we can discover what the "now" is really all about. This is not a manufactured idea that we conjure up. Rather, these conclusions come from real human experience in wrestling with the very issues that are driving us crazy today.

In addition, the pilgrim takes a similar perspective in looking toward the future. The faith-filled person knows that there is always much more to come because history really is going somewhere. The contemporary moments when good and evil are locked in combat are not relative or inconsequential. At some future point there will be a final resolution of these issues, and a verdict will be rendered on each person's life.

The Bible is filled with the conviction that history is moving in a straight line toward a great consummation in the total realization of God's purposes. Human events do not happen in a random or capricious manners as a result of fate. The Bible teaches that a Sovereign God stands behind the scenes, and that in the end His designs will not be frustrated. Those who are part of His plan and live out His will for their lives can anticipate that the future will always be even more full than they could have dreamed.

"Now" is essentially the transition point between yesterday and tomorrow. The past gives us clues to our identity, and the future promises a destiny to each person. Today is not an isolated moment but part of a steady beat in a great celestial symphony that is constantly resounding with surprises and promises. When we begin to hear the sound, a new sense of synchronization is given to our life.

Recognizing this grand design infuses a renewed and enlarged sense of responsibility into what we are doing right now. The way we live and how we make decisions is vitally important after all. Time travelers are deeply involved in getting the most out of every moment of their lives. Right now is to be lived to its fullest potential because it is part of the building blocks out of which the future will be constructed.

Jesus taught a number of parables that underscore this idea. For example, the parable of the talents (Matthew 25:14-30) is the story of a group of people who were given money to invest during their employer's absence. Upon his return they were called to give a strict account of how well they had used the opportunity at hand for business investments. Reward went to the diligent and punishment to the irresponsible. Jesus taught that the future will be highly significant, and that we must consider the present hour in light of what is to come.

GEORGE

Through a number of years of counseling with disoriented people, I have watched the practical results of what happens when this sojourner perspective is applied. I am reminded of George. In the mid-1960s he was the typical dropout flower child of the California scene.

"Man, like it's all going nowhere. I mean there is no point to the action." Drawing deeply on a cigarette, he continued, "The system will suck you in if they get the chance, and you end up a puppet of the middle class."

George was adamant in his position. He could discuss for hours the meaninglessness of American life. Usually he would conclude, "Big Daddy, count me out! The whole thing's going under anyway."

And, in fact, he really was out! Deeply involved with drugs, most of his time was spent rambling around beaches and babbling in bars and coffeehouses. Occasionally he would be aroused to some sort of protest. Generally this was more sport than genuine concern. In the end, he was drifting through his twenties with such personal disregard that at 29 he looked like he was almost ready to turn 40.

At that point a group of "Jesus Freaks" hit him with the whole Christian message. With concerned fierceness they preached biblical passages, one after another. They insisted that Jesus Christ was the answer to his despair and disillusionment. Ultimately he tumbled to the message and fell hard.

Overnight, he turned 180 degrees in the direction of this newfound faith. The story of the changes in his life is an adventure-filled drama. But of greater interest is where George is five years after that conversion. Recently we had this conversation.

"Robert, I need your help in some decisions we are making about a piece of real estate." George was very serious and businesslike in his approach. I asked him why he was involved in a large purchase of land.

"Well, we need a lot of space for our drug rehabilitation program. The kids who come to us need to be isolated from the pressures and forces that got them hooked. So we need to get them out in the country and lost in the trees." Then he became intense: "We have really prayed that God would lead us to the right place where we can help the most kids."

George can't find enough hours in the day to accomplish what he feels is important. He works at a 40-hour-a-week job, teaches several Bible studies, and spends countless hours with teens.

Life going nowhere? Not anymore!

In a similar vein, I've watched bored housewives, affluent and indulged businessmen, hedonistic college youths, and disillusioned divorcees find new joy in living. The biblical perspective completely changed how they felt about their experience of life. Time was tamed!

GETTING THE MOST OUT OF TODAY

Let's go back to the Book of Hebrews for another big clue about what today can really mean. In this simple phrase a radical potential for every moment is promised: "Jesus Christ is the same yesterday and today and forever" (Hebrews 13:8).

While this passage is often quoted as a statement about the Person of Jesus Christ, it is also a promise about today. As He was there in past history and will stand supreme at the end of time, He is always our Contemporary. Each day of my life is a time of keeping divine appointments.

Today is not unhooked from the future. Tomorrow will come, and this same Jesus Christ will be there with more special appointments. What tremendous stability these appointments can give life!

In a rather remarkable way the Apostle Paul applied that insight to the development of his whole life. In his letter to the Philippian church his whole sense of time was expressed in terms of the meaning of Jesus Christ's presence. Through numerous adversities and painful experiences he was able to have a continuing sense of stability.

> *But whatever gain I had, I counted as loss for the sake of Christ. Indeed I count everything as loss because of the surpassing worth of knowing Christ Jesus my Lord. For his sake I have suffered the loss of all things, and count them as refuse, in order that I may gain Christ and be found in him . . . and that I may know him and the power of his resurrection . . . (Philippians 3:7-10).*

Paul can teach us how to have the same power!

The past is put into perspective. Out of human history I can learn about Jesus Christ and discover what God has done. While the past is important, it doesn't have to be glorified out of perspective. Nor do I have to be afraid of incidents in my own history that might fill me with embarrassment. All of the past has the potential of bringing me to Jesus Christ. Even if I have experienced great personal loss, that also becomes acceptable when I can understand how that deprivation brings me to Christ.

The present comes into focus. Knowing Jesus Christ transforms the encounters I have with people, nature, and things. In the present moment my experiences can be gathered together to better gain Christ. And that is not an isolated experience of "trip." Life really is going somewhere, because through Jesus Christ I have a gauge and barometer to measure direction and destiny.

Make no mistake! Nothing is avoided, hidden, or ignored. The present does not become shallow or trite. Paul sees the "now moment" as the opportunity to "share his [Christ's] sufferings, becoming like him in his death, that if possible, I may attain the resurrection from the dead" (Philippians 3:10, 11). <u>Even pain has a profitable place</u>!

The future is given a shape. All of the transition points in life can lead me, step by step, toward a more complete grasp of reality discovered through this Christ. The guest is not just a religious matter but is also a basic insight into what life is intended to mean and where my life is meant to go. Contrary to the current mind-set, everything about our world points beyond today. Sun, moon, and every growing thing anticipates another day and more to come. The pilgrim time traveler has simply discovered destiny: it is Christ.

MAKING NOW COUNT

Now we are really in a position to pull our life together. We can recognize why many people seem so crazy. Long ago psychology discovered that people who constantly live in the past are trapped in their memories. That adjustment is a form of mental illness. Moreover, people who constantly live in the future and out of their fantasies are also disturbed. Therefore, I must conclude that people who live only in the now are caught in a new form of craziness. Their total preoccupation with the contemporary makes them go bananas. Over and against such narrowness are three basic suggestions for finding new fullness for living.

First, you can put sychronization and stability back into your life by refusing to be pushed and propelled through this present moment. Rather, recognize that today is your time of maximum opportunity to really live. Every event of your life can be filled with significance. Sift and shift until you know that the structure of your life is leading you toward a maximum opportunity to "gain Christ."

Second, you need to build pockets of quiet into each day. I have found that I must meet Christ in moments of quiet and stillness if I am to be able to hear Him over the roar of the traffic and the ringing of the telephone. You will have to fight to hollow out such times. You will find not only *Him* but also an ability to keep yourself from being overwhelmed by the rush of life.

Third, expect divine appointments to be kept. Life is not intended to be filled only with a meaning that you supply. When we start to anticipate the intervention of God we are constantly surprised by the fullness that everyday living develops. I often find that through casual conversations or seemingly chance encounters with people an amazing serendipity hides behind their words. In reading books, magazines, and particularly the Bible, divine rendezvous suddenly "happen." What a sparkle these moments give to each day!

In effect, you will be balancing each day against the past and toward the future. Such equilibrium naturally brings stability. And in the process I think you will find that you are becoming one of those special time travelers for whom life is always a great and fulfilling adventure.

3

Shaft Thy Neighbor

"You only go around once. So get all the gusto you can!"

And with that advertising slogan a new lifestyle is promised to us. You can get the gusto from life if you drink the right beer, wear a monogrammed shirt, dance at the swinging disco, etc., etc. The special product, hooked up with the current social cool, can take you a long way, baby! All are critical factors, since you are only going around once. But the most important ingredient in getting the gusto is your lifestyle.

The title of Jacqueline Suzanne's novel *Once Is Not Enough* seems to suggest a haunting contradiction to the new slogan. Strangely enough, the sad demise of her characters just might confirm that verdict. Actually, her best-selling books are about the gusto lifestyle of the jet set. Their plots depict the wild and extraordinary adventures that are possible when money can buy everything.

Apparently many people read her stories because they want to get a feel of what a completely affluent life is like. Yet these books actually give a vivid picture of how people severely damage and abuse each other when the gusto is life's largest prize. Going around once seems to end rather painfully in Ms. Suzanne's novels!

TAKING A CLOSER LOOK

Though the "once-around-gusto-style" is the "in thing," we must look at it much more closely. Contemporary novels and cinema have inadvertently given us some important clues about why people are experiencing instability. I'm convinced that the relentless quest for the gusto is an important ingredient in what is driving us nuts.

Statistically, something is badly amiss in contemporary society. For example, since 1960 the divorce rate has risen by 114 percent! We have the highest divorce rate in the world.[1] Today, *half* of all hospital beds are used by mental patients! The United States is at the top among nations with the problem of alcoholism.[2] Obviously, the whole national lifestyle bears some investigation.

We have observed earlier that a loss of time orientation will cause us to feel unstable. Wild, radical change further increases the suspicion that nothing is predictable and reliable. These social forces combine to make us feel we have flipped, gone bananas, lost our buttons, etc. Unless the now moment is balanced between the past and the future, we will simply go out of kilter.

The gusto lifestyle is actually adding more fuel to the fire because it undercuts stability in a very subtle way. The live-it-up-now idea has ushered in a complete new value system. This new ethic is itself undercutting our sense of well-being. To understand the effect, we must get inside gusto morality.

GUSTO MORALITY

The "once-around" philosophy is built on a new basis for personal morality. A very different approach to human relationships is implied. In fact, we are now involved in a battle over a new consensus about our social behavior. If the now morality wins, you can expect to experience greater instability than ever.

The old national ethic was based on the concept "love thy neighbor." We knew that people didn't practice that ideal all the time or in every situation, but most of us felt that the slogan represented what we really ought to do. So there was strong social approval and there were good strokes when people acted with concern for the other person. The average American citizen liked to feel that both he and his neighbor were basically motivated by what would be best for the other.

The present shift is an attempt to replace the love slogan with a new motto. "Shaft thy neighbor" is the new byword. Expressed in practical terms it is, "Do it unto him before he can do it unto you," because he's certainly going to give you the shaft when the opportunity arises!

Since you've got the gusto coming, you have a right to get it the best and quickest way you can. You have a right to pursue your wants regardless of the cost to other people. I'm suggesting that this new atmosphere is not healthy for human beings. Here are some examples that shape my conclusion.

GUSTO IN ACTION

One of the major crime problems in urban areas today is shoplifting. In recent years an amazing upsurge of petty stealing has plagued businessmen. Are the culprits professional criminals? No, the thieves are middle-class citizens with money in their pockets! Because items were wanted, they were simply taken. The result is that everybody pays higher prices at the counter.

Time and again the newspapers have reported rapes, assaults, and muggings that took place in sight of large crowds of people. Many witnesses watched and did nothing. The police were not even summoned. When the observers were pressed to explain their chronic indifference, the usual response was, "I didn't want to get involved." Behind this explanation was a total lack of concern for others.

Recently in Oklahoma City a young man was peeved at an acquaintance. To express his animosity he decided to play a little joke. He stole the car of this ex-friend and set it afire. He felt that his hostility would certainly justify the little caper. Tragically, two children were asleep in the back seat of the car and burned to death. The gusto got a little out-of-hand.

In a counseling session, I heard the basic problem expressed in the story of a young woman's troubles. Married at 18 and going straight from her parents to a husband, Cathy had a child at 21. Shortly after the birth she got the message that she was only going around once. If she didn't grab the gusto quickly, opportunity and her figure would soon be gone.

Cathy simply made herself available to the opportunities at the office. No question about it—once wasn't enough. A stream of boyfriends rambled through her life. While there was no end to the excitement, the result wasn't at all what she expected.

No longer was Cathy able to relate to her husband. She felt confused about her emotions toward the little boy. But equally significant was the personal confusion going on inside her.

"I feel like I'm sliding off the edge and can't hang on much longer," Cathy explained.

Noticing the rather hysterical look in her eyes, I asked, "You're under a lot of pressure?"

"Well, not from people around me. It's pressure inside." She paused and reflected a moment. "My life is so out-of-control that I feel kind of crazy a lot of the time."

Her conversation, the avalanche of the irrational in the newspapers, and the bizarre events that seem to be becoming common place all merged in my mind. The lines of a poem by W.B. Yeats floated up from my memory. This relentless search for gusto had turned his words into fulfilled prophecy:

> *Turning and turning in the widening gyre,*
> *the falcon cannot hear the falconer;*
> *things fall apart; the center cannot hold;*
> *mere anarchy is loosed upon the world.*[3]

Shortly after the center is lost, we become irrational.

I'LL GET MINE FIRST

The "if it feels good, do it" mentality is not going where

the advertising promised. In the end, the result is alienation, loneliness, boredom, and the anxiety that is born out of emptiness. The anarchy around us and within us demands that we get a much clearer picture of what this new ethic means. Let's begin by understanding how we got to this new place.

Dr. Roger Blackwell, professor of marketing at Ohio State University, studies America's changing lifestyles. He is particularly interested in why societies change. Dr. Blackwell has discovered that what children experience as deprivation they strive for as adults.[4]

Therefore, the Depression Era produced adults whose primary concern was economic security. Their children became the interpersonal generation. Overemphasis on material things sent this generation in quest of more-human values. While their parents were concerned with thrift, this group wanted to spend everything right now.

However, the following and current generation is building an "immediate consumption" mentality, and the result is the "I'll get mine" attitude. Blackwell concludes that this represents a disinterest in the good of larger society because of a total preoccupation with personal needs. Of course, the ultimate social result bcomes a form of anarchy.

In effect, the first generation's sights were set on bread alone. The next generation's vision was set on plenty of bread *now.* And the resulting descendants couldn't care less if anyone else was fed.

Dr. Francis Schaeffer also clarifies why we have changed. In the "love-thy-neighbor" era, individual lives had deep significance and work was very valuable for its own sake. As American society lost a Christian consensus, these values no longer directed people's lives. In their place, two new and very different ideals have become predominant. Schaeffer has discovered that personal peace and affluence now mold and direct contemporary life:

Personal peace means just to be let alone, not to be troubled by the troubles of other people . . . to live one's life with minimal possibilities of being personally disturbed. Personal peace means wanting to have my personal life pattern undisturbed in my lifetime, regardless of what the result will be in the lifetimes of my children and grandchildren. Affluence means an overwhelming and ever-increasing prosperity—a life made up of things, things, and more things—a success judged by an ever-higher level of material abundance.[5]

On these two pegs, the "I'll-get-mine-first" people hang their values and dreams.

Is Schaeffer correct? Well, listen to the TV commercials and read the ads in magazines. The advertising industry in America certainly seems to believe ardently in personal peace and affluence. A whole host of products are offered with the assurance that their usage will guarantee one or both of the golden goals.

Even church organizations have recognized the drawing appeal of these values. Some ministers have built empires on the promise that following their personal teachings will either increase your wealth or grant you peace of mind through blocking out a needy world. Unfortunately, these opportunities are very shortsighted. Once these utterly self-centered ideals are embraced, a whole ethic of selfishness follows. This ethic is not only pulling things apart but is causing people to lose the spiritual center that is necessary for personal stability. Let's look further at how this moral anarchy is operating on the mainstreet of everybody's hometown.

HOW TO GET THEM FIRST

In order to pull off this new lifestyle it's extremely important that you *not* feel guilty. Apparently guilt short-circuits people who are out to get the gusto. So it's crucial that you be able to shaft your neighbor without having bad feelings. Therefore, a new type of literature is here to instruct us how to deal emotionally with what we do to other human beings.

Recent best-sellers give clues about how persuasive these ideas have become. Robert Ringer's *Winning by Intimidation* and *Looking Out for Number One* were major national successes. Wayne Dyer's *Your Erroneous Zones* stayed in the number one position for a number of weeks. Michael Korda's *Success And Power* were also big sellers.

All these books have obvious similarities. First, they start with a smattering of practical psychology that deals with personal adjustment. To this they add some helpful insights on how to get along better with your girlfriend, boss, etc. Then the whole mix is coated with a thick philosophical layer of utter self-centeredness. The constant maxim is, "If you feel bad it's your own fault." What's important is getting what you want and believing you have a right to the result, regardless of the cost.

For example, *Your Erroneous Zones* teaches that rights and wrongs get in the way of our happiness. Dyer believes that those categories don't exist and are meaningless.[6] You should learn to live without such inhibitions. Moreover, you ought to learn how not to feel tied down and responsible. "Psychological independence means total freedom from all obligatory relationships."[7] Worrying about right, wrong, and responsibility can only breed guilt and dependency. Dyer and friends want to deliver you!

From his practice as a psychologist, he shares a practical application of this thinking. Helen came for counseling because she could not endure the affair her husband was having. She was distraught and anxiety-ridden. But Dyer was quick to point out that the problem was really all Helen's fault.

He suggests a multitude of reasons for the affair that

should be understandable and impersonal to Helen. She should just see the situation as something happening between two people with no relationship to herself. "The upset rests solely in Helen."

So tough to you, Helen! If you will just buck up and be an "I'll-get-mine-first" person, the infidelity won't bother you at all. The sense of shame is all in your head!

Dyer seems to know nothing about the pain of betrayal or has never experienced the emotional significance of deep caring. Either way, these solutions are madness called by another name.

Because these how-to books have a superficial foundation of psychology, their philosophy tends to slide by unexamined. Yet what is suggested in thse books has the ultimate emotional effect of pulling things farther apart and enthroning nonsense at the center of the decision-making process. Their suggestions are offered in the name of stability. The result is disaster.

THE ETHICAL BABBLE

An analysis of these ideas and this literature was given in a very unexpected place. Since these books have been such big financial successes, *The Wall Street Journal* ran an analysis of their contents. Daniel Henniger noted that the common goal of these books is to give everyone an absolution from all guilt. Generally this is done by suggesting that you develop your own value system that seems to best fit your own needs. Henniger notes that morality seems to have very little to do with anything for these writers. In the end he concludes that these writers "constitute a modern ethical babble."[8]

I conclude that the result is even more destructive than that. When getting the other guy first is a serious objective, then real harm is going to be done to the society and to individuals. The ultimate expression of the problem came out in a book published by Financial Management Associates of Phoenix, Arizona.

Practical tips include "how to do it to your employees

so you can keep them smiling on low pay" and "how to maneuver them into low-pay jobs they are afraid to walk away from." As for taxes, they will show you how to hide your money and ultimately to "get out of trouble using the bankruptcy laws to cover your tracks and save your . . . ." There are a host more of these insightful ways to give everyone in sight the shaft!

Yeats prophesied that anarchy would be loosed upon the world. Financial Associates have the battle plan, and Ringer and Dyer have sounded the trumpets, but Yeats is the only true sage in the bunch; he understood that the real result will be that "things fall apart; the center cannot hold."

IRRESPONSIBILITY WILL DRIVE YOU CRAZY

It is obvious that what has been traditionally considered responsible is being seriously questioned. Moreover, irresponsibility is being openly advocated. It is precisely that emphasis that may be the most devastating attack on our personal stability. When the whole gusto package develops into a dropout mentality, the end result is not personal satisfaction. To the contrary, this is the soil from which bananas grow and instability flourishes.

While working with the emotionally disturbed, psychiatrist Dr. William Glasser discovered that what had been generally called mental illness might just as accurately be labeled irresponsibility. The failure to take control of one's actions and decisions will lead to an immobilized emotional condition.

Dr. Glasser discovered that we all have a basic human need for relatedness and respect. While we often call this need "being loved," the experience of personal affirmation is built from these two components. It is not possible to have any sense of genuine relationship or personal regard unless we are "doing what is realistic, responsible, and right."[9] Glasser believes that "morals, standards, values, or right and wrong behavior are all intimately related to the fulfillment of our need for self-worth."[10]

His conclusion is simply that people who are irresponsible will become ill. Emotional problems or illness are the result of acting irresponsibly.[11] People who are out "shafting their neighbor" are actually at work tearing down the very center that is necessary to hold themselves together. Even on the basis of nothing more than human psychology, the gusto ethic is extremely unhealthy.

As a therapist, Dr. Glasser knows that there is no lasting feeling of self-worth unless the individual is maintaining a "satisfactory standard of behavior."[12] While there may be some debate about what is a universally accepted norm for personal morality, Glasser believes that acting below such a level of morality will undercut the personal worth which we all must have to be mentally healthy.

That means we must be worthwhile to others to be able to be worthwhile to ourselves. In the end, following Financial Management's principles of business or Dyer's personal morality will produce people who flip out or go bananas. The current social priorities of personal peace and affluence are actually a major part of why we feel disoriented. Rather than gaining peace of mind, we are generating internal confusion.

The great American psychologist Dr. O. Hobart Mowrer has come to similar conclusions. To be a truly whole person is not so much a matter of deeply personal insight or self-understanding. Moreover, Mowrer does not even feel that the neurotic person needs more freedom to just "be himself." Rather, only through a deep experience of *commitment* beyond ourselves will we find the stability we seek.[13]

So what the popular "improve-yourself" books advocate (retreating from moral and spiritual commitment) leads to the exact opposite of what they are promoting. Long ago the philosopher Spinoza observed a similar conclusion. He noted that we don't think of greedy or excessively ambitious people as insane, but just annoying. Yet their preoccupation with money, possessions, or fame is actually a form of insanity.[14]

Dr. Erich Fromm has pointed out that if multitudes of people should consider a vice to be a virtue, that in no way changes the truth. Moreover, if millions of people develop the same form of mental illness, that will not make these people sane![15]

People who are no longer responsible with alcohol are called alcoholics. Perhaps we ought to label people who are irresponsible with the control of their money and possessions "thingaholics." People who abuse other people's lives are clearly "egoholics." And the "get-mine-first" people are "gustoholics"!

Now we have a new and clearer perspective on why currently popular lifestyles seem to leave us disoriented and emotionally empty. Clearly we need much better alternative. Let's look again at the method of those time-traveling pilgrims.

A STABILIZING ALTERNATIVE

Sojourners have long understood why the "you only go around once" style is hollow. It's no surprise to them when the gusto path turns out to be a dead end. Over 2000 years ago another best-seller detailed the results of that route. The writer wrote:

> *I said to myself, "Come now, I will make a test of pleasure, enjoy yourself." But behold, this also was vanity. I said of laughter, "It is mad," and of pleasure, "What use is it?" I searched with my mind how to cheer my body with wine. . . .*

And then he details how he set out to satisfy every desire of his ego and ambition. Actually, he tells us he surpassed all his peers in total accomplishment. But in the end he concluded:

> *Then I considered all that my hands had done and*

the toil I had spent in doing it, and behold, all was vanity and a striving after wind, and there was nothing to be gained under the sun.

The book is named Ecclesiastes, and it is in the Bible. These quotes are from the second chapter. The point of the whole volume is to describe the final results of a life based on nothing but the quest for personal self-centered satisfaction. We remember the book best for its woeful conclusion about where it will all end: "Vanity of vanities, says the preacher, vanity vanities! All is vanity" (Ecclesiastes 1:2).

The biblical sojourner has learned to search in a completely different direction. In the last chapter we discovered that stability requires keeping a sense of balance which recognizes the importance of both the past and the future. For the present moment to be fulfilling, we need to have a personal sense of accountability about our lives.

When Jesus was asked about accountability, He gave the most important guidelines by which people could live: "You shall love the Lord your God with all your heart, and with all your soul, and with all your mind," and of next importance, "You shall love your neighbor as yourself" (Matthew 22:37,39).

Though this guideline is being debated in the marketplace, Jesus' answer is still the most effective direction for emotional stability. Integrity based on a commitment to God and others produces lasting satisfaction.

Dr. Mowrer has suggested that mental health is found through real personal commitment. He suggests that the words of this old hymn are basic to our sense of well-being:

Holy Spirit, Right Divine, Truth within my conscience reign: Be my King, that I may be firmly bound, forever free.[16]

That is the conclusion, not of a religionist, but of a

clinical psychologist. Developing personal integrity and living beyond yourself is the stabilizing alternative that is needed today.

SATISFACTION THAT LASTS

Will such integrity and commitment stand the test of stressful times? Well, we have rather extensive records of one pilgrim who spent his life not only in such a quest but in telling others how they could live successfully. We know him as the Apostle Paul. He wrote a letter to some friends who lived in the ancient city of Philippi. In this letter he expressed the opposite conclusion from the writer of Ecclesiastes:

> *. . . I have learned, in whatever state I am, to be content. I know how to be abased, and I know how to abound; in any and all circumstances I have learned the secret of facing plenty and hunger, abundance and want . . . (Philippians 4:11,12).*

Interestingly enough, that was written in a prison, and the theme of his letter was joy!

Paul was saying that satisfaction is not found in what you have or do not have. Fulfillment is not in what you want or don't want. If satisfaction is a new car, next year I have to get *another* new one. If fulfillment is having the most magnificent house on the block, the guy down the street builds a better one. It goes on and on.

Paul concludes his teaching with the ultimate answer: "I can do all things in Him who strengthens me." Out of his integrity and commitment to a life of love, lasting satisfaction was really possible.

Paul realized that the character of God puts a balance on our wants. The personality of God is like a giant frame that surrounds our existence. All kinds of impulses, wants, and wishes roll around in our heads. But correct balance is restored by the boundaries of this framework. In the final analysis, love is a far better test of what is valid behavior than the gusto which strikes my fancy. When the character of God provides our boundaries, and the intentions of love are the arena for our actions, we are guided by dreams, ideas, and ethics that are permanent in every age. Such stability insures satisfaction.

1. *The Oklahoma Journal,* "Divorce Rate Is Almost Unbelievable," Tom Broden, December 3, 1977.
2. Eric Fromm, *The Sane Society* (Rinehart & Co., 1955), Chapter 1.
3. William Butler Yeats, "The Second Coming," in Yeats, *Collected Poems* (New York: The MacMillan Co., 1924).
4. *The Daily Oklahoman,* "How Trends In Life Styles Affect Families," Sharon Dowell.
5. Francis Schaeffer, *How Should We Then Live?* (New Jersey: Fleming H. Revell Co., 1976), page 205.
6. Wayne Dyer, *Your Erroneous Zones* (New York: Avon Books, 1976), page 153.
7. Ibid., page 199.
8. *The Wall Street Journal,* Daniel Henniger, October 11, 1977.
9. William Glasser, *Reality Therapy* (New York: Harper and Row, 1965), page XIII.
10. Ibid., page XV.
11. Ibid., pages 13-16.
12. Ibid., page 10.
13. Ibid., page XVI.
14. Eric Fromm, *The Sane Society* (Rinehart & Co.), page 13.
15. Ibid., page 15.
16. Glasser, *Reality Therapy,* page XVI.

Part II

And Then I Flipped Out!

The Loss of Personal Identity

A Crazy Little Conversation With Sam

Sam came to talk with me about finding enough money to help support his family during a difficult time when he was out of work. I felt I might be able to help him find a line of work that would have long-range possibilities.

"If you could choose, what would you really like to get out of life?" I asked.

He looked rather startled. After a pause he replied, "Well, really nothing. There's nothing that particularly interests me."

Nothing! I was amazed!

"There's nothing that is really worth worrying about," Sam said. "If I set some goal, I may just change my mind and want something different tomorrow. Since that's possible, I just don't see any reason to worry about having a purpose in what I do."

His answer really astonished me. Surely there was some sort of challenge I could give him. So I asked him more about his future plans.

"But where would you like to be in ten years?

What would you hope to have accomplished by then?" I probed.

Sam reflected awhile and then said matter-of-factly, "I might like to be living on top of a mountain somewhere just looking out a window. I guess that's about it. I sure wouldn't be interested in having some executive job or a lot of money in the bank."

I protested, "How can you be so directionless?"

"Well, I believe the whole world is going to blow up in 20 years anyway." Sam was very sure as he continued, "Striving doesn't get people anywhere or make them happy. I just want to live from one day to the next."

Since I knew that Sam was a bright young man I wanted him to see the contradiction in his situation. "But look at your bills—and what about your child?"

"Oh, it will all work out somehow." And with that he just walked away as if the original problem was no longer important.

For several minutes I thought about our whole conversation. Doesn't someone who wants nothing, is going nowhere, has no ambition, and has no hope for the future have to be considered a little bit crazy? Though Sam was not bizarre or in any way berserk, isn't such purposelessness really irrational?

There are millions of people who think exactly like Sam.

4

Help! I've Lost Me!

After the first day of boot camp, two young Marines found themselves standing naked in the showers at 11:00 at night. Eighteen hours earlier they had arrived in their faded blue jeans and long hair. One fellow had come with a magnificent mustache and the other had sported long, flowing sideburns.

Now, after the most physical day of their entire lives, they could hardly stand up. Their heads and faces were completely shaved, and the scorching heat had left them badly sunburned. Their ears still vibrated with directions and commands that a drill instructor had screamed all day.

One shivering, naked, peeled young man turned to the other and asked, "Who did you used to be?"

Multitudes of people floating across each others' lives are asked the same question. In airplanes, over a cup of coffee, across the dinner table, people ask each other, "Who did we used to be?" Before the times smashed past us like a steamroller, we were sure there was a clearcut identity somewhere. Now it all seems to be misplaced.

In those few moments when we are truly alone, the same haunting thought often comes rambling by. Maybe there is a feeling of desperation as that strange question comes bubbling up from underneath our anxieties and uncertainties. We find ourselves thinking, "I don't know what's happened to me, but I think I've lost myself."

Frequently after a divorce, one of the parties will drop by my office to talk about how it feels to adjust to his or her new situation. Far more often than I would have guessed, their identify was tied to the roles they lived out in their marriage. With the familiar patterns and routines gone, their stability has vanished too.

John faces another kind of problem. For 20 years he was happily employed by a major petroleum company. Then they automated and he was replaced by a machine. Where is he going to turn for work, and how will his family survive? Equally haunting are his questions about the future of a worker in an age increasingly run by computers. His identity is badly shaken.

Alice has just discovered that her college-age daughter is living with her boyfriend. She raised her daughter according to all the convictions and values that her parents had instilled in her. Now the daughter is rejecting those values. Moreover, Alice's 35-year-old best friend confides that she too is running around on her husband. In the avalanche of contradiction and change, Alice has become confused about morality, and at age 38 she's not sure where she's really going.

Bewilderment caused by change has created an inner confusion that eats away at personal certainty and security. In these times, identity has become a critical question. The young Marines in the shower are speaking for multitudes of people. We have lost ourselves and we're not sure where to look next.

HUMPTY DUMPTY TIMES

Earlier in this book we looked at the impact of changing times on our sense of stability. The forces that are crumbling the social structures are also affecting our personal well-being. *External* pressure is a major problem for our sense of well-being.

Now we shift the focus and look at the *internal* side of the problem of stability. While identity has always been a difficult need to meet, today's adjustments are much more complex than ever before. When all the social rules are rearranged, we discover that we are being changed as well. That impact on our identity can be most disturbing.

Large portions of our identity come through the reflections that are mirrored in our many relationships. Friends, employers, teachers, mates, children, enemies, and associates act as a many-faceted mirror. Through these interactions we catch glimpses of who we are. When the mirror cracks, the picture is distorted.

In our Humpty Dumpty world the fractures run in every direction. The values and ideas that make us tick are in a continual tension with what we see on television and read in the papers. Novels and movies keep asking us questions and issuing challenges. Indeed, change is being demanded every day of our lives. Friends and acquaintances may be of no help at all in getting stabilized.

The deep crevices in social values and the cracks in contemporary morality are causing the identity of many people to be quite tenative. The bent reflections we are seeing in today's cultural mirror only add to our personal instability.

Consider two controversial subjects: homosexuality and abortion. A scant ten years ago there was absolutely no debate about the right and wrong of these issues. The homosexual was hidden, and no one would admit to having a sex-change operation. But change has set in, and now we may not be sure at all how we relate to these issues.

Recently I was part of a television discussion on homosexuality. The other guest was a "gay" person who was advocating that his sexual identity be recognized as an acceptable alternative lifestyle. He proclaimed that homosexuals should not seek therapy in order to develop a "normal" sexual identity. While he assured me that he had found a satisfying life, he kept alluding to severe emotional stresses he faced. I pointed out to the young man that he himself was a convincing argument for a considerable confusion about his identity. Though he had come out of the closet, he was a long way from home!

SALLY

Sally was caught in a similar bind. She came to talk because her mother had "sent her." The mother had insisted that Sally have an abortion, and now she was concerned about its effect on Sally.

She began, "I don't really need to talk to you. For some reason my mother is worried about how I'm taking all of this."

"Well," I asked, "how do you feel about the abortion?"

"Oh, fine. It really wasn't a bad experience," she reported matter-of-factly. "It didn't bother me at all. I had no problem and everyone was so nice. It didn't bother me at all."

"And your mother," I asked; "she feels okay about the abortion?"

"Well," Sally paused a moment, "she really seemed confused and uncertain. She has the problem." Then she added again, "It didn't bother me at all."

I noted that Sally seemed to be trying to reassure herself. So I asked further about why her mother wanted her to see a counselor.

"I just don't know," Sally stated.

By the end of the conversation she casually added that she did cry a lot and couldn't sleep well even though "nothing bothered her at all."

Subsequent visits disclosed that, since the abortion, Sally was no longer sure what kind of person she was. While being told the abortion had no meaning, she couldn't accept this idea. In a word, she had become troubled about her identity.

The homosexual and the young girl are experiencing their own internal backlash. External change hasn't helped but rather *intensified* their problems of identity. While denying any problem, they both were feeling the pain of a fractured age that had increased the distortion of their own personal identity.

These conversations led to the same conclusion: "Help! I've lost me!"

TELL ME IT ISN'T SO

An interesting thread of continuity runs through these conversations. In different ways these troubled people are trying to deny some facet of their identity. But trying to ignore any dimension of reality only increases the problem.

We have already discussed how the past is necessary for maintaining personal stability. One's personal history is even more critical in establishing a sound sense of identity. Good or bad, acceptable or unacceptable, we need our own immediate history and its roots in order to find ourselves.

Once again the changing social order produces problems. Contemporary life is highly transient, leaving the impression that nothing is permanent. Everything is temporary and disposable. We don't stay anywhere long enough to establish a real past.

Americans have become a nomadic people. Recently an executive of the IBM Corporation quipped that the company's name really means, "I've Been Moved." In *Future Shock*, Toffler describes the consequence that this mobility has on the new corporation executive. As he moves, he may leave everything behind, including his wife and children. In his new location, he simply develops a new family. Consequently, the children left behind find their normal identity problems compounded.

The whole of society appears to be at work denying that the past has any value. The result obliterates the deeply significant work of tradition, location, and relationships in helping us establish who we are.

Often we don't like what we can remember. Millions of Americans try to escape the personal data that they have on hand. *The Wall Street Journal* recently noted:

> *People by the thousands are tied up in analyzing their emotional horoscope, cycles, transcendental meditation, communal nude bathing, and other forms of letting it all hang out, or utilizing any method that gives a promise of escape from themselves as they are.*

"Tell me it isn't so" takes on an incredible variety of shapes. Kinky religions, esoteric cults, science of the mind groups, and Oriental religions have swept across America. Often parents are baffled in explaining the lure that these strange groups have for their children. But if you explore the answers of the youth, the reasons aren't hard to discover. In a society that has cut them loose from the past, they are unable to accept the legacy that their parents offer.

Their parents are no different, except that the elders' form of escape is more subtle. An experiment in Detroit holds a big clue for us. One hundred twenty families were offered 550 dollars to turn off their television sets for just once month. Ninety-three families responded that it would be impossible to live without the tube!

One lady reported, "My husband would never do it because he comes home from work and immediately drops in front of the TV. He gets up only twice. Once he eats and the other time he goes to bed."

The big box with the flickering tube has become our retreat center. Sitting in the reclining chair is our new national prenatal position. The continual diet of trivia blocks out what we don't want to face. Enough of Channel 9, 5, and 4 will help us believe "it isn't so." So rather than grappling with troubling questions, we postpone the inquiry until the rerun season—and then we forget about it.

MORE BANANAS GROWING HERE

When personal identity is frazzeled like the frayed end

of a hemp rope, our stability will be just as unraveled. To be so unstrung will make us unstable and unsteady. If we feel we have lost ourselves, we have a clue as to why we often feel just a little crazy.

Our new slang descriptions are quite adequate to describe what we are feeling every day. "Flipping out" may be a more accurate description for what we feel than is a psychologist's diagnosis!

Actually, a whole science of psychiatric practice is in a turmoil over proper definitions for mental and emotional disturbances. Radical social change has also confused clinical practice. Social workers, psychologists, and psychiatrists no longer agree over the meaning of neurosis.

Since 1973, a new version of *Diagnostic and Statistical Manual of Mental Disorders* has been in the planning. This book is the major guideline for psychiatric diagnoses of problems. Chain-smokers, coffee addicts, marijuana smokers, and shy people are listed in the proposed revision as being clinical catagories. The lines between stability and disorder are quite blurred, and the authorities can't agree about new guidelines.

The debate reflects our confusion over what is normal. When the experts can't decide, our dilemma is increased. So we must explore further why we are all in such a quandary.

Three basic ingredients compose the soil from which instability has grown and flourished. The denial and retreat from reality that is rampant today has cultivated and fertilized this garden in which we have lost ourselves. We must probe beneath the soil-like climate of modern living to get a really good look at our emotional roots. Until the foundations are sure, we have no insurance against becoming a Humpty Dumpty!

1. *The Loss of an Adequate Model*

The first ingredient in our instability is the loss of a clear-cut picture of what constitutes a real person. We have lost a decisive human model with which we can identify. The lack of agreement about what represents a healthy normal human being is part of the definition problem that currently plagues the psychiatric and counseling sciences.

We are caught in a strange dilemma. There is a sense in which the question about our identity is becoming rather absurd. After all, there is really an obviousness about the question "Who am I?" Have we forgotten our father's name? Has the place of our birth or educational experiences slipped our minds? Was there never a hometown in which we grew up? Unless we have amnesia, how can we miss the implications?

What if one evening at supper I should discover that my good and faithful sheep dog had learned how to talk? In the midst of a bite of steak, suddenly I am astonished to hear him address me for the first time.

With his head to one side, Chevzas begins, "Robert, I have been observing you for some time. Most of the time you don't act like a dog. Then again, often you do!"

In consternation I might respond, "Good heavens, you can talk! What do you want?"

Rather philosophically, the enormous dog answers, "I would like to know you in greater depth, Master. Tell me who you really are."

Through my mind races thoughts like, "Does he think I'm a cocker spaniel in pants?" "What shall I say to him?"

Clearly this is all nonsense. Certainly, any of us ought to be able to clarify who we are in relationship to a dog! Yet we have a great deal of difficulty in clarifying who we are in relationship to each other and to our society.

Our problem is that we have lost our point of reference. So badly has our model of humanness been blurred that within the scientific and academic communities there are now many people who could not easily give clear-cut answers to my talking dog.

Prior to the twentieth century people would not have had any difficulty in answering my dog. They were not troubled with this confusion. For example, consider the

Greeks and their philosophers. Herodotus, Aeschylus, Socrates, etc. all explored the principles of beauty, truth, history, and meaning. Fearlessly they probed for a core description of reality. Yet they did not need to ask who they were.

An investigation of the medieval period will reveal the same thing. Read the works of men like Peter Lombard, Abelard, and Thomas Aquinas; they were trying to find a meaningful connection between the events of their lives and eternity. Though living in a rather dark and uninformed era, they weren't preoccupied with questions about what people ought to follow in order to be truly human. Identity was no problem for them.

Move forward into the succeeding periods of history, and you will discover their concerns. When you read Alexander Pope, David Hume, John Locke, or Rousseau you find a deep probing into how society and governments ought to be constructed in order that human life can flourish. But they did not ask who they were.

The difference between the people of the past and our present situation is that they had a reference point that gave them a meaningful starting point. Their identify was shaped around a model that automatically answered many of the questions that trouble us the most. Because they did not need to deny their origins, they could very easily have conversed with my talking dog. We will return in a few pages to clarify what that model for identity was.

2. *The Loss of an Adequate Method*

The second ingredient in our instability is the loss of a path that will lead us into and through our experiences, and then back out to answers that are final and satisfying. Most of the contemporary approaches to finding our identity describe how we should investigate our past; but the paths they suggest generally lead only to more questions.

With the advent of the Freudian era a particular approach was laid down which the twentieth century has brought entirely. The psychoanalytic method of self-understanding has become accepted as the principle way to establish personal identity. While this discipline of modern psychology can be valuable in helping us deal with our emotional problems, it has not been adequate in leading us to a sense of identity that brings emotional stability.

The self-analysis method of self-discovery operates like mining for minerals deep within the earth. We begin by going deeper and deeper into our emotional makeup. The solution to finding our identity is promised somewhere down near the bottom of our inner selves. We must backtrack on the hidden side roads of our childhood and developmental experiences until we hit paydirt. So we delve deeply into the murky, unconscious side of our personalities until "who we are" pops out and can be recognized.

Discovering and walking through the back roads of your memory is by no means an unprofitable experience. In fact, uncovering and dealing with the residue of yesterday is not only worthwhile but essential to personal growth. Lots of hangups get cut down and set free during such journeys. While getting a handle on our behavior is extremely important, I've found that this quest just doesn't lead us to the promised gold mine of selfhood that we seek.

Trying to find the essence of who we are by this method is like trying to discover the meaning of an onion by peeling away the layers. As a child I was fascinated by what I might find at the center of a big yellow onion. I can remember carefully prying back layer after layer in search of the magic something that made it grow.

Though playing with onions brought tears to my eyes, I was determined to find out the secret of its life. Always the search ended with the same disappointment. I would have a tabletop filled with layers of peelings, but nothing more!

Onions are just onions. The whole *is* more than the

sum of the parts. The secret to its vitality lies in its unity. Fragmented onions don't really tell you much of anything.

No matter how many tears are shed along the way, peeling back the layers of experience won't lead to final conclusions about who you are. You can find out a great deal about your fears, doubts, and reservations, but when you hit the center you are in for a peeled-onion experience. There is no magic hidden there to surprise and reward your efforts.

The real you is much larger than any of your parts. The sum total of your experiences produces a "you" that is something more than can be found in any portion of those previous events. Expecting to find a surprising and mysterious answer somewhere deep in the center of your subconscious will only cause you to miss discovering the more obvious identity that is to be found in what you are as a total person.

Mining for personhood in the deep, recessed caverns of our emotions has proven hazardous for multitudes. ESP, "pop" psychologies, transactional analysis, marathon weekends, etc. have promised shortcut routes for travelers going inward for personal direction. However, the analytic method has just not been adequate in finding our lost identity.

3. *The Loss of an Adequate Perspective*

The third ingredient in our identity confusion is an inevitable result of the first two problems. We must have some sort of definition that gives us direction for everyday living. When there is nothing beyond ourselves or little within to guide us, we inevitably turn to some role we fill as the answer to our identity.

When we don't have a psychological or philosophical answer, we give ourselves a sociological solution. You can almost see the wheels turning in the minds of struggling people. "Ah ha! I know who I am! I am what I do."

Consequently, our meaning and purpose is derived

from a role or combination of roles we play in everyday life. While there are valid grievances and injustices that have prompted the Women's Liberation Movement, the identity problem furnishes much of the emotional energy behind the hostility of many within the Libbers ranks. Many women have had no sense of identity except through some role they perform. When those roles are threatened or destroyed, a blow is struck that cuts self-assurance and the stability to the quick.

Too often the answer to personal identity becomes: "I am a wife; I am a husband; I am a salesman; I am a teacher; etc., etc." But when these particular functions are gone, the person is lost. We lose ourselves when we cannot find anything higher to tie to than our performance. The sociological perspective is just not adequate.

A combination of these three ingredients—a last model, method, and perspective—provides a climate in which fragmented people flourish. Rather than having any sense of unity, we simply become a component of many pieces that sometimes work together and often don't coordinate at all. The many pieces force us to conclude that we have lost the whole and ourselves. Such an identity crisis will cause anyone to be at least a little crazy.

In these times of social turmoil we are pushed toward instability not only by the changing bases by which identity is established, but also by the way in which the importance of the past is denied. Further, our escapist patterns of living cause us to avoid the issues that could help us the most. Since we have almost a genuine model with which to identity, and since the method of self-discovery offered us is defective, it certainly isn't a surprise that we feel "zonkers" so much of the time!

RECOVERING THE PATTERN

Once we know what is wrong, we have come a long way toward being able to reestablish what is right. Being able to define the elements that seem to pull us apart will help us in pulling ourselves together. Actually, the diagnosis is part of the cure.

But more help is on the way! Let's go back and pick up the clue from the history of previous centuries. Remember, prior to the twentieth century the question of identity was not the problem that it is today. The people of the past did not worry about identifying with a model that could give them self-understanding. There is a distinct contrast between them and us.

The difference is that today we begin the search with ourselves, whereas their quest for personhood started by looking beyond themselves. We tend to make ourselves the measure of all things, but they looked to a much more transcendent guideline. A faith perspective rather than a psychological method was their beginning point in understanding why they were.

Generally, they believed there was a mold from which they had come. Believing they had been created in a certain image gave them specific direction to what would otherwise be unanswerable questions about their identity. Most of these ancients began their quest with this perspective:

> *Let us make man in our image, after our likeness; and let them have dominion. . . . So God created man in his own image; in the image of God he created him; male and female he created them (Genesis 1:26,27).*

The Bible provided them with the pattern needed to clarify what a genuine human being was meant to be. On this basis they knew who they were.

What a difference this design made! They had a starting point and a concluding goal for their personal search. All kinds of difficult questions could be pursued because they knew that God had given them dominion over the whole world, and that included themselves. Yet there was no great mystery about what they were as persons. As they considered the image of God, or

"Imago Dei," they had the ultimate source for personal identity.

So their approach to self-understanding operated something like this: their starting point was the conviction that God had made them to be uniquely like He is. On that basis they could look around at their relationship to society, to governments, and to each other and project what culture ought to be. They could describe accurately the conditions under which human beings would be genuinely happy and fulfilled.

If they chose to go within themselves, it was not a descent into an abyss filled with unknown corridors leading to undefinable destinations. They had no fear of getting lost within themselves and coming back as lost souls who had been changed into different people by the journey. Because they started with the Image of God, in the end they returned to the same pattern. Knowing their origin and their ultimate destiny insured them that they would not lose themselves.

THE LOST IMAGE

In sharp contrast, the twentieth century has lost touch with the Imago Dei. Because we have nothing to look at but ourselves, we have lost a real reference point. As we travel into the murky, unconscious side of life, we have made our self-discoveries the ultimate gauge of who we are. This introversion is where we lost our way!

But here is some good news! The Image-of-God pattern is like a rope that is lowered to the miners lost in their own emotional mining projects. The Imago Dei is a light that can shine down into the dark caverns in the recesses of our minds. This model will provide the unity needed to pull together the many diverse facets and fragments of our personhood. When we start to identify with the Image we will begin to know who we are.

The pattern will also produce the path. A more adequate method follows when we begin to look in the right direction. It is primarily a matter of asking the right questions.

Thomas Howard, professor at Gordon College, suggests that a major reason for our not establishing a sound sense of identity is this very question that we keep pursing. He suggests that asking "Who am I?" automatically reflects our dilemma. This is the wrong question to ask if we are going to get a right answer about ourselves.

Howard notes that if anyone ever had the right to that question, it would have been Adam. Immediately after God moved to create humanity, Adam came on the scene. But nowhere in the Genesis story do we find this solitary human being ever reflecting on who he was.

Rather, in his primal state of fulfillment, Adam is occupied with two things. He has been given the world to subdue, and he has been given another person with whom he can relate. His work and his companionship make his life complete. His sense of satisfaction is possible because he asked a very different question.

Instead of the identity question "Who am I?" he asks of his creator "Who are You?" His method of self-understanding was a continuing inquiry into the nature of God. With profoundness, the writer of Genesis tells us that the real key to understanding what we are to be is found in discovering the way God is. The rest of the Bible reveals progressively that the image and nature of God are knowable. So the path to pulling our fragmented lives together is the pursuit of God's pattern for us.

REGAINING PERSPECTIVE

The difference between this century and previous times is that the people of those times talked to God and we talk to ourselves.

In learning how to ask "Who art Thou?" we too can recover the perspective needed to find ourselves once more. Rather than finding our identity by crawling inside, this new question lifts us above our contemporary situation. This perspective will lead us to the more satisfying answer.

If the Imago Dei is our guide, what design is being suggested? What does God's image look like? How am I supposed to be like God? What should I identify with in order to know myself?

Through the centuries a number of key descriptions have been given of God's reflection in us. One idea has been that the ability to think is the key to our identity. Certainly, rationality is a gift that makes us distinct as human beings. Yet just being a more reasonable and reasoning person doesn't satisfy our emotional need for inner direction.

Other thinkers have pointed to creativity as the essential link between us and the Creator. This school of thought believes that as we are being creative we come the closest to achieving our status as real persons. The creative person does indeed discover a deep inner sense of satisfaction and wholeness, but some of the greatest artistic minds have not known peace or stability. They too have been haunted by misplaced identity.

Though rationality and creativity are good clues, there is more to the Image of God. The critical ingredient is found in a deceptively simple phrase: "God is love" (1 John 4:8). The most complete description we have of "the way God is" is encompassed by the word "love."

Being motivated by and acting out of love brings us the closest to being like God and becoming ourselves. Through loving we are able to realize God's image unfolding in us. As we love, our fractured self is healed and genuine wholeness is achieved. Loving has its own special way of removing the craziness from our lives and leaving in its place a genuine sense of stability.

Because the word "love" has been so badly misused in recent decades, we must make sure our definition is the same one that John used. In the rest of his paragraph he spelled out what the love of God is:

In this the love of God was made manifest among us, that God sent his only Son into the world, so that we might live through him. In this is love, not that we loved God but that he loved us and sent his Son to be the expiation for our sins (1 John 4:9,10).

Love is self-forgetfulness. Rather than being absorbed in self-interest, love turns openingly to the needs of others and reaches out even to the point of self-sacrifice. As we forget ourselves in loving others we actually find ourselves.

In the first part of this chapter, I described people who were utterly preoccupied with themselves. We have seen how popular self-help literature encourages "looking out for number one." Yet the result is always the same: the self-preoccupied people are the very people who are going bananas!

In contrast, Jesus taught that "he who loses himself will find himself." Losing oneself on behalf of good and the needs of others leads not to *loss* but to the very *gain* necessary for personal stability.

There is nothing abstract about how we can do this. When I identify with Jesus Christ and pursue life through Him, the direction that love should take becomes clear. Since the Imago Dei was perfectly demonstrated in Jesus Christ, by studying and following Him I have a very human model of what complete and full personal identity is like.

In finding the Image of God, I find myself.

5

Getting Your
Head on Straight

Question: Why is the Image of God so hard to find?

Answer: Because we get most of our religious instructions at the movies!

Whether at the theater or at the television set, meaning, purpose, and an experience of the mystery of existence are conveyed to the masses through the media. While watching actors reconstruct a celluloid version of reality, we are led to conclusions about what makes the universe tick and who we are.

This is especially true for those people who firmly believe in self-worship (which is perhaps our major American religion). Ours is not an irreligious age; rather, in our era we believe in gods who are different from the traditional God. Today's deities are generally found in the mirror!

THE ME GENERATION

Tom Wolfe called the young adults of the seventies the "Me" generation. With the advent of the Human Potential Movement (ESP, Transactional Analysis, Sensitivity Training, Encounter Groups, etc.) and the onslaught of mass personal introspection and emotional explorations, he has concluded that we have produced a new national narcissism. The pervasive emphasis on self-awareness has become part of a religious devotion to loving one's self.

Consequently, a complete religious system has evolved which has replaced the Image of God with the image of self. The current worship of "me" comes with a complete ethic, and it imports a weak and defective but definite sense of identity. However, such an inadequate basis for self-understanding only furthers personal instability.

"Me" worship has adopted the basic premise, "If it feels good, do it." Being in love with ourselves is considered to be automatic justification for whatever we want to do. The "me" ethic believes that the *desire* is sufficient reason for our actions. Moreover, the uninhibited and unrestrained lifestyle is recommended as the most effective route to self-realization.

Self-worship proclaims that the pursuit of the fulfillment of our impulses will lead us to self-discovery. The idea is that as we let it all hang out, the real us will emerge, fulfillment will be instantaneous, the drabness of life will be erased, and happiness will overflow. Unfortunately, the attempt to put the ethic and promise of self-worship into practice has produced high percentage of today's national nuttiness! We are simply being sold a defective faith.

A recent major motion picture gave us detailed instruction in the new religion. *Saturday Night Fever* is the inspiring story of Tony, a 19-year-old high school dropout. He is contrasted with his neurotic mother, unemployed father, and disillusioned brother. By pursuing self-worship, Tony is clearly more enlightened than his elders.

Tony works in a spray paint shop. At night he drives around town like a maniac, scaring people to death. He spends a great deal of time admiring and worshiping himself. The worship center is his mirror, where he endlessly combs his hair and obviously loves what he sees. The big moments of self-disclosure and fulfillment come at the Saturday Night Disco.

Tony is the Disco King. Whether on the dance floor or outside in the back seat of his car, he is the masterful conqueror of all. His world of seduction and dancing is a practical demonstration of the ethic and the identity acquired through self-worship.

Insight is reinforced as we are given explicit religious instruction through a conversation between Tony and his brother, a Roman Catholic priest. The priest is quitting because he can no longer believe in the Church or in the Christian faith. He assures Tony that, in today's world, right or wrong is found only in what we want to do. Doing anything because *we* want it makes the action okay.

RELEASING THE REAL YOU

"Me" worship holds the conviction that the "Real Me" is hidden at the center of my personality. The idea is that there is a little person within me who, when released, will rescue me from the colorless life that I feel I lead. Expressing this "Real Me" is believed to be the key to fulfillment. Devotees have confidence that such a self-discovery will reverse the erosions which come with age.

Though we love that reflection of ourselves in the mirror, often we find the image far from satisfactory to us, and with the passing of time the likeness becomes less adequate and beneath our expectations. The idea of the "Real Me" suggests that perhaps there is actually a miniature Farrah Fawcett, Burt Reynolds, Gertrude Stein, Picasso, John Kennedy, etc. lurking below the surface. That "other person" promises to be the true one.

Tony and his self-worshiping friends believe that the only thing keeping the "Real Me" from popping out is repression. Parental hangups, sexual inhibitions, church prohibitions, antiquated moralities, etc. all combine to suppress the true person locked up inside. When these confining ties are cut, self-realization is accomplished. Consequently, on Saturday night we can turn into a Tony and be ready to swing.

Contemporary psychology suggests that identity can be discovered from the clues found within our past. Self-discovery becomes possible when we are able to draw conclusions about the meaning of our personal history. In contrast, "Me" worship essentially changes the focus of the identity quest. Instead of searching the past, we are to turn the present into an emotional springboard for self-expression. Uninhibited emotional release is the method which will reveal identity. The problem is that this gospel of self-indulgence just doesn't work!

Like fun-house mirrors that distort the true reflection, people who have looked for this "Real Me" miss the very thing they are seeking. In fact, trying to be this mysterious "other person" often turns into a masquerade.

We may first try on one image and then, with time, change into quite a different appearance. Like clothing styles that change, so personality takes one shape after another.

I attended art school with a middle-aged woman who was a complete devotee of the self-expression approach to personal discovery. Janet had not been able to find any lasting sense of satisfaction with her life. She was convinced that the "Real Me" only awaited the right moment of full self-expression.

JANET

During the year before I met her, Janet had pursued yoga and health food as the route for realization of her identity. Before that she had also tried Christianity. Initially Janet thought the church offered escape from her unfulfilled life. However, upon closer examination the Christian life required too much discipline for her taste.

The last time I saw Janet she had moved on to theater for her salvation. In addition, she was taking disco lessons and divorcing her husband.

After she told me the story of the family breakup, I remarked, "I'm sorry to hear about your troubles at home."

"Oh, don't feel bad," she responded. "The whole thing has been coming for a long time."

"You've been incompatible for some time?" I queried.

"No," Janet said slowly; "we really had a pretty good relationship. The trouble was that Jack and the children have held me back all these years. When I was into painting, all the responsibility held me back. So now that I'm truly free, I know I can really begin to express myself."

As the conversation ended, I wondered what she would be trying next year!

Obviously, such continual shifting can become its own form of craziness. The end result is a feeling of nondirection.

THE ME MYTH

The idea of the "Real Me" fails to impart a sound sense of identity for a basic and simple reason: the whole concept is based on an utter myth.

Margaret Halsey touches the nerve of the issue in an article entitled "What's Wrong With Me, Me, Me." She described what is really behind the looking glass:

The "self" is not a handsome god or goddess waiting coyly to be revealed. On the contrary, its complexity, confusion and mystery have proved so difficult that throughout the ages men and women have talked gratefully about losing themselves.

She concludes that the quest for the self god only results in turning our backs on the honest knowledge that we can have about our identity.

What do we really find within ourselves? The core of our personality is a complicated, contradictory, paradoxical maze of drives, impulses, needs, and desires that respond to and rebound from whatever the five basic senses conjure up for their consideration. A personality model contrived to look like a "miniature human being" lurking behind our thoughts is totally misleading.

A better mental image of our unconscious realm would be a wild, vine-covered, dimly-lit virgin forest. The paths are extremely difficult to travel because they are covered with fallen logs and debris. The inner trails keep coming to the edge of deep, dark, foreboding caverns. Lurking at every bend of the road are unseen presences which we often sense are monsters and wild beasts. You certainly cannot disco your way through such a forbidding place! Within each of us is an untamed jungle.

Long ago, Sigmund Freud recognized the facts about this disordered maze on the underside of our thoughts. In *Civilization And Its Discontents* he discussed the struggle which must happen to make our primitive self produce constructive results. Our native impulses are unruly and disorganized. He concluded that good actions are possible only through considerable discipline and channeling of what lies inside us. Even Freud recognized that "letting it all hang out" did not necessarily lead anywhere.

Consequently, "Me" worship feeds the least constructive side of our nature. By mistaking the contradictions and paradoxes of our personalities for the "Real Me," self-worship tends to unleash the very qualities that ought to be the most disciplined.

THE BETTER PATH

To get through the forest, *you* have to set the direction. Getting your head on straight isn't a matter of letting the impulses rule. Rather, the task is to mold and discipline our drives and desires to conform to the directions we have set for ourselves.

I'm not suggesting that gold is not hidden within those deep crevices and recesses of our own being. But, as for any precious mineral, the reclamation is possible only after the hard work of disciplined extraction. Far from worshiping ourselves, we must recognize our severe limitations and our need for marshaling our forces. This cannot be done except by imposing a higher design upon ourselves and by insisting that the inner maze conform to the better paths we have chosen.

While certainly not a popular idea today, the key to self-realization is *discipline.* No forest yields easily to the bulldozer, and much less to the happy wanderer. The unconscious realm of drives, impulses, and desires is an even more formidable problem for every human being.

Countless millions of people lead drab, unimaginative lives because they have constantly traveled the paths of least resistance. Without plan or intention, they wander through the world looking for magic moments that never come. Actually, their own contradictions and paradoxes rule their lives. Without mental discipline, they live the same directionless lives of the characters in *Saturday Night Fever.*

Rather than restricting, discipline releases potential. I have discovered that creativity is at its best after diligent practice. Genuine, spontaneous expression just "happens" *after* discipline is imposed on impulse.

No great painting, book, or musical work has ever just "happened." Only after the arduous labor of beating back the paradoxes and contradictions within each of us can our best abilities be pulled together and focused on the work at hand. Superimposing a higher image on one's self is an utter necessity for discovering the best that is within us.

MY NEW VISION

For several years I studied watercolor with Michael Bache. The paintings of this Italian immigrant always have a fresh, spontaneous fascination in their shape and form. Moreover, Bache could achieve this effect in a remarkably short time. After a painting lesson, I asked him how long it might take me to get this special sense of light into my pictures.

Bache put down his brushes and mused for a moment, "Oh," he said, "It takes about 20 years and 30 minutes."

Writing has helped me see, with even greater clarity, the necessity of such discipline. Frankly, I did not have any particular interest in becoming a writer. With a college degree in art, I had a much greater interest in painting and ceramics. Then, Fritz Ridenour, a friend who is a successful religious writer, urged me to explore painting with words.

My drives and impulses rebelled at the whole idea. When I sat down at the typewriter, my sense of light wanted to enjoy the pictures on the wall. My sense of taste urged me to go to the kitchen for popcorn. My sense of smell sensed that the spring air outside was far more inviting than the stale air around my desk. Something inside my ears longed to turn up the volume on the stereo. "Letting it all hang out" meant bolting for the door, grabbing some watercolor brushes, and expressing "Me!"

Fritz had a higher idea. His insistence began to impose the image of "writer" on my thinking. I forced myself to put paper in the typewriter and stare until my fingers obeyed my better thoughts. The forest of distractions did not yield easily, but the "writer image" forged a path through the vines and branches of impulse.

His vision became my vision. With discipline, a new sense of identity began to come forth. There was no little man with a pencil hiding inside me. Rather, disciplined direction forged a superior, more satisfying path than I would have imagined. An identity happened because I set the direction from which it could arise.

Such valuable paths are not easily found, because modern advertising is constantly guaranteeing us easier alternatives. Motivational researchers have thoroughly catalogued what appeals to "Me worshipers," and they have a product for every wish. The right deodorant and toothpaste do the trick. Testosterone hair oil and estrogen face cream will release the "Real Me." Body remolding machines will bring forth the real us in 30 days or less. Any product is preferable to discipline!

Of course, such promises are nonsense. Hair oil will not get your head on straight. Identity doesn't come in a bottle or from a squeeze tube. Neither can it just ooze out of the center of our personhood.

The better path leads us back to the need for a direction from beyond ourselves in order to unlock the mystery of who we are. A more lofty image is needed than our own reflection in order to maximize the potential within. The exchange of the self-image for the Image of God is a poor bargain.

Indeed, "Me" worship has made the Imago Dei difficult to find. In addition, being unrealistic about human nature and retreating from self-discipline has increased the problem of self-discovery. Actually, these same ingredients produce much of the instability, causing many of us to be more than just a little crazy. Therefore, something more must be said about the divine Image as a guide to identity.

THE PUZZLE AND THE PROMISE

A secular society immersed in self-worship has a difficult time understanding how the Image of God can affect identity. God-talk seems totally foreign to the age of psychology and sociology. Man we know about; God we have only heard about, and that is a distant memory.

We are convinced of the animal quality within ourselves. Our affinity with the zoo can be grasped much more easily than with heaven! In fact, the last four decades have indelibly etched on our consciousness an image of just how much of an animal we can be. Nothing from the jungle has the savage capacity to sow destruction and pain like the homo sapien. Mai Lai, Kent State, Dachau, Belsen-Bergen, saturation bombing, Hiroshima, etc. are historic testimony to the wild fury of unleashed human impulse.

Today we are keenly aware of human frailty. While

noble and altruistic actions are far from unknown, a lurking suspicion of our innate self-centeredness and manipulative nature haunts modern man. We have become pessimistic about humanity.

Consequently, people who only look at themselves are never able to get the full picture of their promise and potential. The Imago Dei seems reserved for religious people and saints. At best the idea sounds irrelevant, and at worst it seems to suggest repression of our wants and desires.

Nevertheless, this puzzle still contains the promise of self-fulfillment. Intuitively we know that humanity is meant to be more than animal. We naturally aspire to live on a higher plane.

In fact, the very way in which we feel driven to find our identity bears witness to our inward realization that something more than bestiality is meant for us. Unconsciously as well as rationally, we know there is another half of our personhood that we must find in order to be whole. Our desire for the "Real Me" is a silent yearning for what is in reality the Image of God. Fulfillment lies in not giving personal and social definitions to this wish but in recognizing what God has already given us.

HIS GIFT IS LOVE

God's great gift is love. In loving, our personalities reflect the personality of God, and our basic identity can be established. In fact, the real "us" isn't discovered in *knowing* ourselves as much as it is in *loving* like God does.

For many of us, the hardest part is in believing that we are loved by God the Father in a total, unconditional way. Since most of our experience has been with people who have manipulated and used us, we have grown up feeling that our value is contingent on performance. So we have difficulty in realizing the complete way in which God loves us. In turn, we have quietly and subtly decided that our own value is quite limited. Again, the notion that God completely accepts us seems almost unimaginable. Not being able to recognize our worth, we have a difficult time actually loving others and appreciating their value.

We need to first accept the fact that God *does* love us completely and totally. For many people this may seem impossible. Often, being loved by God is an idea that we must live with for many years before the implications finally filter into the core of our being. But the historic proof of God's love is in the life and death of Jesus Christ on our behalf. Because I accept the truth of His action, I have ample reason to know I am loved.

When I am able to believe in the possibility of His love, I can then seriously start to explore rebuilding by His Image. This approach reverses the way in which we generally try to find ourselves. Rather than the answer being in where I have come from, I am able to look in the direction of where I am going. I begin to build positively on what I *can* be.

Just as my friend convinced me of the possibility of accepting the image of "author," so when I am convinced of God's love I can accept His Image as the ultimate design. On that basis I am able to pull my impulses and needs together in a new and creative direction. Even more, accepting His love imparts a tremendous new sense of self-worth. His Image is a guarantee that my value as a person does not have to be contrived. Possibly for the first time, I discover that I can be fully at home and at ease with myself.

FINDING THE IMAGE

If we are going to conform the inner person to that Image, we need to have the shape in a clear focus. The Bible suggests that Jesus of Nazareth is the complete expression of the Image of God. In looking at His life, teachings, and actions, we discover exactly how the Image of God is to be expressed in the most human of terms.

Therefore, as I know Him I can begin to take on the identity that I seek. The Image and love of God actually is not an abstract idea at all. Through Jesus Christ I can discover exactly what form this Image takes in everyday life. Particularly, His teachings and actions detail how this oneness with God's design can be expressed.

As I latch onto the person of Jesus as my Guide through the maze of vines and debris inside my inner forest of unconsciousness, I am able to pull my impulses and desires together into a creative unity. Automatically I sidestep the confusion and instability that comes from following the impulses of the moment.

The Bible describes this process as "receiving Jesus as Lord." The idea is that I recognize His life and death as having particular and singular significance for me. I accept that what Jesus did conveys the most total and final possible picture of God's love for and acceptance of me. Moreover, from this point forward I will let Him be my Model of what an authentic human being is. The patterns for relationships, self-expression, and values that I discover in Him will become the guidelines for living my life. Through that decision I can actually identify with Him and begin to take on the new identity that I need in order to find stability in an unstable world.

THE NEW LIFE

On this basis I begin to grow a new life. The better shape starts to unfold like a budding plant, and good results are absolutely guaranteed.

> *Just as you received Christ Jesus the Lord, grow out of him as a plant out of the soil it is planted in, becoming more and more sure of the faith as you were taught. And your lives will overflow with joy and thankfulness (Colossians 2:6,7 Phillips).*

Rather than looking inside myself for the final answers, I relinquish and release my life to be shaped by what I see in Him. Consequently, the "Real Me" is best developed by pursuing Jesus as my Lord. Inevitably I begin to cultivate the best potentials I have.

You will find that there is a basic common sense about this whole idea.

Much of the time we are keenly aware of our limitations. If we are not, the people around us will help us get the picture. Sooner or later we are forced to recognize our inadequacy in fulfilling the dreams and hopes that we have for ourselves. In those moments of insight we become our own harshest judge. As we lament our inadequacy, we feel the pain of our own failure. The pangs of disillusionment come in the moments in which we fully realize the inadequacy of self-worship.

As great a writer as Ernest Hemingway was, he came to his own final despair. He described himself as having become like a burned-out light bulb without a source of electricity. Shortly after that realization, he committed suicide.

H.G. Wells began his writing career spinning stories about the miracles of science and the all-conquering power of the human mind. He had great optimism about the potential of humanity. Yet at the end he wrote "Man at the End of His Tether."

In *Passages,* Gail Sheehy detailed the developmental stages that all adults pass through as they mature. The changes in adult thinking, she concludes, reveal a picture of how our illusions about ourselves crumble and give way to a continual recognition of our frailty. Time pays few compliments to our ideals of superiority.

What we carry inside has very limited adequacy in carrying the freight of our total life experience. Common sense demands that we find something bigger and beyond ourselves to guide us. If we are going to have an enduring stability, it must be added to our lives.

An astonishing contrast is found in those people who have "received Jesus Christ" and gone on to allow their lives to grow into that identity. Not only do they find stability, but they make lasting contributions that leave the world a better place.

LES MISERABLES

Victor Hugo, the great French writer, expressed in his classic novel *Les Miserables* his convictions about the profound result that comes from establishing an identity through Jesus Christ. The story of Jean Val Jean is the story of the transformation of a broken, disillusioned man into a magnificent human being. Imprisoned for the most minor of crimes, Jean's treatment is so degrading that he is reduced to a wild creature who survives by being nourished on hate. He lives purely by his impulses and desire for revenge.

After having escaped from prison, Jean encounters a Roman Catholic Bishop. The kindly, loving priest takes the dirty, disheveled fugitive into his home and treats him as an equal. Astonished by such gracious treatment, Jean inquires into the priest's motives. Humbly, the Father explains that they are both brothers in Christ, and he acts out of Christ's love.

Unable to comprehend such an explanation, Jean steals away in the night after taking the valuable household and church silver. Immediately he is caught by the police and brought back to the rectory. Once the priest identifies the stolen items, Jean will go back to the dungeon.

To the surprise of all, the priest welcomes his brother back. Yes, the silverware was his. But he had been expecting Jean back: he had forgotten something. As police and prisoner watch in astonishment, the godly little man hands Jean the silver candlesticks as well and wishes him Godspeed.

The police leave, and Jean Val Jean breaks into uncontrollable tears. Love and compassion have broken through the walls of hate and fear that have controlled his very existence. As he begs to understand what is happening to him, the priest speaks the words of absolution and forgiveness in Christ. Beneath the crucifix, Jean becomes a new man.

The rage and malice that have filled his soul slip away, and a new identity is forged after the Image of God. The rest of the novel is an exhilarating story of courage and nobility that arises out of the ashes of dissolved despair. Victor Hugo's story is a demonstration of the transformation that comes through a renewed identity established in Christ.

THE POWER OF THE IMAGE

Through 20 centuries, countless millions can attest to the power of this Image to establish an identity that imparts genuine personal stability. Here is a recent example of someone who personally discovered what Victor Hugo described.

Judy Pomano is a housewife in her early forties. We were having a casual conversation when she began sharing the details of the transformation in her own stability. Her story began when Judy discovered that she was an illegitimate child.

At 27 years of age, she stumbled onto the truth about her birth and parentage. To her chagrin and astonishment, Judy discovered that the family's story of her birth, early childhood, and family structure was not true at all. Though the facts were concealed in a well-meaning attempt to protect her, the truth was all the more devastating when it broke so suddenly upon her.

With the effect of a hurricane in the night, all the familiar moorings in her life were blown away. While the walls of her family world tumbled, her identity crumbled and fell apart. Judy's self-understanding was suddenly gone. She stood stripped before the storm and left without a sense of meaning or destiny. Because of the deception, she felt she could not trust anyone to tell her the truth. Her life began to break up into little pieces and drift out from under her; there was no identity to pull things back together.

A counseling process was begun. The therapist, who was a Christian counselor, attempted to apply the dynamic of meaning in Jesus Christ to her emotional problems. Judy had been raised with a knowledge of who Jesus of Nazareth was, and she had known people who expressed His love.

While she doubted the dependability of people in general, she sensed that the love of Christ was a foundation that would be solid. Slowly and carefully she began to reconstruct an identity centered around the love of God. Her personhood began to evolve a new pattern after the Imago Dei. She was rebuilding a center around a new definition of love. Strength and stability slowly but permanently returned to Judy's life. Her new stability was more than she had ever known previously.

Having journeyed to the center, struggled with her fears and disillusionments, disciplined them to fit a better pattern, and surfaced a whole person, Judy was ready for a normal life again. She was soon to discover that the intense pain of self-discovery had brought an unexpected reward: a special gift had taken shape within her; a unique empathy and insight into the loneliness and fright of abandoned people was now a significant part of her consciousness.

Judy had acquired a natural understanding of the inner world of foster children. Intuitively she had a feel for the emotions of the abandoned child. A special warmth and compassion flowed from her heart to children who desperately needed to be coddled and cherished. Love came naturally to Judy now.

She and her husband, Dick, began opening their doors to abandoned children whom no one else wanted. The couple found that they were uniquely suited to handle the overwhelming emotional demands of battered children. Little frightened waifs of the night discovered, as did Jean Val Jean, that the gift of love can replace terror with hope. Judy demonstrated that the Image of Love could create a new identity that would heal. The Pomanos have now raised eight children.

As I sat in her living room, intrigued by her story, a little six-year-old girl came home from school. This tiny first-grader had been a severely battered child. Sharon was born to a teenage drug addict. The young mother had so severely mistreated her daughter that at the mention of the mother's name Sharon would break into tears and scream in terror. But on this afternoon, that world of fear was far behind her.

Sharon crawled up on Judy's lap and hugged her neck with glee. Looking around her shoulder, she smiled and proclaimed with pride, "This is my mommy." Sharon and Judy had both been born twice, and the last time was in the shape of love.

6

Going Nowhere Is
Going Crazy

Getting lost leaves you with the strangest sense of disorientation. As your inner gyroscopes whirl out of control, you feel your sense of perspective turning into a strange state of craziness.

One morning at about 1:00 A.M., I found myself on a back street in Mexico City, utterly cut adrift and floating without a compass. Though I was walking back to my hotel, I felt like a ship lost at sea with a sky shrouded in fog.

Having spent a great deal of time in Mexico City, I was very familiar with the streets, boulevards, and landmarks. In fact, I felt no qualms about walking through back streets even at this late hour. The evening performance of the Ballet Folkloric had been extraordinary, and a nice walk was in order. It seemed like a good idea to take a shortcut and to bypass the longer and more defined route down the Reforma thoroughfare.

While I knew that Mexico City had grown up out of the development of the old colonial sections that had merged together as suburbs do today, I had forgotten what these changes had done to street names. An avenue might start with one name, but as it continued across another colonia, it would suddenly change to an entirely different designation without explanation. Consequently, you could cross a street you were seeking and be completely deceived by an unfamiliar and unexpected name designating an ancient and unsuspected colonia. My shortcut took me through one of these undesignated areas, causing me to pass my street without even blinking an eye.

After walking about two miles out of the way, I began to have a suspicion that something was wrong. Nothing looked familiar, and all the usual landmarks had disappeared or seemed distorted. A creeping, haunting sensation began to cross my mind. It was 2:00 at night and I didn't know where my hotel was!

If the last of the late-night taxi drivers had not happened by, I suppose I would still be wandering around that city of 14 million people, trying to act nonchalant while terror dilated my eyes. I got into the taxi and slumped back, hoping he would rescue me from the asphalt forest.

Not until the exact moment when the driver pulled up in front of the hotel did I have any sense of bearing. As I stepped to the curb and blinked, a strange mental rearrangement began to revolve in my head. Slowly north, south, east, and west started to appear on my mental map again. Stability started to settle in.

My shortcut experience left an indelible impression on me: going nowhere is going crazy! When your sense of orientation is distorted, you feel more than just a little nuts. If the underpinnings that hold identity together slip, the resulting sense of lostness will be experienced as an overwhelming experience of emotional instability.

DETOURS

Today millions of us awake each morning to discover that someone has changed the road signs of life without notifying us. What had formerly given us our bearings and clarified our identity has been removed. We're sure that we're on the same path that we were traveling when we went to bed the night before. Yet on this particular morning we have become lost. What had meaning the day before is now without value, and panic sets in.

Our identity is critical for a basic sense of orientation. When some facet of our self-description dissolves, so does stability. Consequently, the death of a child, the divorce of a mate, the loss of a job, the reversal of our financial position, or the radical change of living conditions can become our own contemporary impenetrable forest.

In addition, when our identity is obscure and undefined, we are in a position that makes us feel highly susceptible to instability. Previously we may have functioned quite well because we had a general idea about who we were and had not been confronted by any serious challenges. However, in a period of chaos the lack of explicit knowledge about our inner resources can have the same effect as lost direction.

In contrast, the ability to reach deep within our mind and find a fundamental, bedrock sense of personhood allows us to absorb the pain and disruption of a life detour and to continue successfully on our way. When we are able to be in touch with the definitions that have shaped our personality, we can endure what would otherwise be overwhelming stress.

Actually I am suggesting that our identity can take two possible forms. One form is an *implicit* general sense of who we are. Any functioning person operates out of an often-unexamined presupposition about his values, aspirations, and goals. This latent identity is for each of us our "common sense" about how things ought to be. The problem is that our implicit identity and common sense may be riddled with fallacies. Therefore, we need to develop the second form that is open to us.

An *explicit* sense of identity is a personal and particular definition that we have brought out in the open and examined. It is a conscious awareness of ourselves that we have openly decided is true. We can verbally express this description of ourselves and cling to it in a crisis. For example, the Image of God can be acknowledged and be understood to express the highest truth about ourselves. We can choose the Imago as an explicit definition of our identity.

People who don't get lost in their own life crisis generally operate with an explicit sense of who they are. Strength and endurance come from an explicit set of personal definitions that can be called on when the issues of living have turned murky and obscure.

In the next few pages we are going to explore the need for developing an explicit sense of identity and how that can be achieved. In Chapter 4, the problem of confusion over the source of identity was discussed, and the Image of God was suggested as the personality model we need. Chapter 5 explored how contemporary myths about the "Real Me" have made it difficult to get personhood into clear perspective. Now we will consider how a well-defined and explicitly stated definition of personhood can become an internal compass that will give us bearing regardless of tomorrow's detours.

In order for the Image of God to offer us personal stability, we must have keen awareness of our own need to clarify our sense of identity. We ought to be able to state our self-understanding in terms that we can talk about and relate to someone else. We must define the guidelines that have formed our values and ideals. Without these explicit definitions, all of the answers suggested up to this point will only be academic.

DEFINING REAL LIFE

Once an identity has been examined and uncovered, it can then become a compass that will operate even in the dark. Defining who we are is literally an exercise in building personal stability. Explicit personal definitions equip us to turn our detours into scenic side-trips leading to maturity.

Alex Haley has given us dramatic instruction in the power of claiming one's true personhood. For much of his own life he floundered about without a sense of direction. Unable to get a handle on his destiny in life, he failed as a son, husband, and father. Because he was going nowhere, he failed to have the emotional tenacity to fulfill those roles.

New direction began to develop as he began finding an explicit identity as an author. Still troubled, he pushed on to an even more ultimate grip on his personhood. Out of that quest was born the powerful best-selling novel, *Roots.*

Two scenes from the television version come to mind as I remember what a dramatic difference personal definition made for Haley through discovering his personal roots. These episodes depict the positive and negative sides of clarifying one's identity.

During his Coast guard career, he developed a close friendship with another black person who was older and higher in rank. A father figure, John taught Alex about life. Filling in what Alex's churchly upbringing didn't supply, he exposed him to "the other side." In time, a deep affection matured between the two men.

Near the end of their service time, they drifted into conversation about themselves. Alex expressed his quandary about his identity. He shared with John his desire to know more about who he was. John matter-of-factly told Alex that a man could live his whole life and grow old never knowing who he was.

A shudder of dread must have run through Haley in realizing what the implications of such a statement could be. In John he could see depicted the multitudes of nameless blacks who had trudged through life without a sense of meaning or destiny. Their implicit sense of identity had not been strong and lofty enough to carry them past hardship to triumph. Alex Haley could not settle for such a life.

In total contrast, his novel ends as he has found his way across the ocean and back through the centuries to the ancient African village of Juffure, where he has reason to believe his family had their origins. The legends of their ancestor Kunta Kinte have guided family conversations for generations, and now he is on the verge of discovering the truth about his mythical forefather.

As the ancient griot, who has all the memories stored in his mind, slowly peels back the layers of the entire history of the tribe Kinte, Alex listens intently. Suddenly the story unfolds of how one Kunta Kinte disappeared in the forest. In utter glee Haley leaps to his feet. Now Alex has the image to complete his identity and make the definition explicit. He has found the old African! Alex has also found himself.

I have watched the same sort of experience happen for many people through the help of an organization called Adult Adoptees. People who were adopted as children find that the questions of identity have not been resolved for them. Although they in no way repudiate the love or care of their adopted family, they simply have the same compulsion that haunted Alex Haley. They need the additional definitions from the past to feel completed.

KNOW YOUR HERITAGE

Once an identity is explicit and can be held before our eyes, it has already started to operate as a gyroscope. Though we may be turned upside down by contemporary events, this internal sense of direction will seek its own true course. Without such a mechanism, we may not be able to recover a sound direction after a personal disaster. Much of today's craziness is the product of inevitable conflict from which the victim has not made a real emotional recovery. Often this is directly related to the lack of any sense of family rootage.

The problem of an obscure family identity is not just a difficulty of blacks and adoptees. The entire American nation has been struggling with an identity crisis at least since the early 1950's. One of the first writers to recognize our dilemma was Will Herberg. In *Protestant, Catholic, Jew* he detailed the identity problems of an immigrant people who had been cut loose from the national moorings of their past and had not really jelled around a new definition of who they are nationally. We are a nation of descendants of immigrants, and original-ly the old countries gave us a sense of explicit identity. However, as time has passed, all that is left of those origins is their religious residue.

Herberg recognized that the old religious heritage had molded into a bland, vague, general sense of religiosity called Protestant, Catholic, or Jew. These religious groups did not impart a strong, abiding sense of identity. Rather, for many people,they had become simply a passing part of the social scene. Consequently, the American religious scene in the fifties was not a source of explicit identity.

The hidden significance of Herberg's observations became clear in the sixties. With widespread disillus-ionment over racial injustice and the Vietnam War, millions of young people could not find meaning in the title "American." One obvious consequence of the lack of heritage was the hippie movement.

The intergenerational family has been lost for many Americans. No longer do we know about the cement that once held us together with our past. Without that knowledge we are emotionally plopped down in time like an American in Mexico City on an unnamed street at 2:00 in the morning. Heritage, pride, and tradition are no longer available to clarify for us what ought to be. *Coming from nowhere is like going nowhere.*

Moreover, increased mobility has multiplied the problem. Statistically, American families have been moving across the county line once in every five years. The moving rate is constantly increasing to the point where relationships in the immediate family are tenuous and sketchy. Not only are grandparents dis-tant, but even fathers may be unknown as sources of direction and definition.

There is no mystery as to why the television version of *Roots* maintained an all-time record viewing au-dience. Americans were not only intrigued by how Haley found an explicit family identity; unconsciously they were thinking about *themselves*. Intuitively we know that personal definitions do make an enormous difference.

THE LABEL PRODUCES THE PRODUCT

The description of one's identity makes such a difference because it is a form of self-fulfulling prophecy. Our personality labels not only tell us what is inside, but they also have a strangely powerful way of describing what we are going to be. These identity labels are the motivators that start us moving somewhere.

Once you have developed an explicit description of yourself, you have written out a label that you can paste on your future. You will be definitely shaped by what you believe is true about yourself. I can absolutely testify from my own experience as to the potency of what self-discovery can lend to a renewed sense of well-being.

At age 17 I stumbled onto an experience that pasted a new label across my tomorrows. Without realizing what was happening, an explicit self-understanding was imparted to me that literally produced a new and different person.

My own sense of identity had always been a problem. In fact, I carried with me an implicit self-understanding that was based on a great deal of negative feeling.

I was different. Clearly, unmistakenly, and inescapably I was different; and being different spells confusion when you are a child trying to sort out your identity. As I developed into adolescence the difference only seemed to be magnified and the self-worth diminished. My father was six feet four inches tall and bald. My mother was above average in height. Both were of a decided fair complexion. In contrast, I was small and dark, and I had more hair than the average monkey. In any family lineup, the viewing could only produce one conclusion: I was different.

So the inevitable, universally asked question was, "Where did he come from?" The family answer was always, "Oh, he's adopted." It was an honest, forthright attempt to settle the misgivings of all concerned. But it actually confirmed only one thing: I had to be explained, for I was different.

Growing up in a small, western Oklahoma town compounded my sense of being misplaced. My village had an unusual social system that was essentially based on the ability to play football and to letter in the sport. As the leaves turned gold and tumbled down, the local citizenry turned red and became more than slightly irrational over the results of the gridiron encounters. The ability to go forth into the high school gladiatorial contests was essential for affirmation and a place of acceptance in the social scheme of things.

You guessed it—having lots of hair just didn't add enough weight to make the right difference! I weighed 125 pounds and didn't even make a good tackling dummy. In short, I could not achieve anything that I felt was significant enough to give me real worth. The implicit identity I carried hidden in my most sensitive thoughts had moved from confusion to a confirmed feeling of inadequacy. Being different carried the silent connotation of being small and limited.

MELVIN MUNN

With that orientation firmly planted in my mind, I happened across a man named Melvin Munn. One of the outstanding public speakers in America, Mr. Munn had been invited to come to our community and speak to the public schools. He had the capacity to mesmerize vast audiences, leaving people motivated and excited. The Kiwanis Club had paid Munn's expenses to tell fantastic jokes and subtly steal into the minds of little boys like me who needed a new sense of their possibilities.

At 2:00 p.m. a special assembly was called and the school student body was herded into the auditorium.

Knowing that teachers were posted at the doors killed my idea of sneaking out the back door and cutting school for the malt shop. Reluctantly I came slouching into the gathering. This was the era of the white T-shirt, blue jeans, and greasy hair, when a look of indifference was totally cool. That afternoon my cool look was about five notches above my level of motivation.

Due to the delay in trying to find an escape, I was forced to take a seat on the very front row; that definitely was not cool. Nevertheless, I settled into the chair feeling trapped by the whole situation. To my surprise, I was immediately captivated by this magnetic man.

Melvin Munn used words like a spider weaving a web. Each phrase, innuendo, and anecdote drew you further into his point of view. The listener was disarmed, captured, and devoured by his ideas. I found myself excited and deeply awakened by his description of what was possible in any one of us. I returned to class stunned by the rhetoric.

I was sitting in English class contemplating the whole event when the principal's voice came over the intercom speakers calling me down to his office. Immediately I was defensive. I knew it had been two days since I had done anything worth a trip downstairs.

Walking into the office, I immediately protested, "Listen, I'm not going to take the rap for something I didn't do. Whatever it is, I'm really clean this time."

"Okay, Wise!" the principal said with a tone of disgust in his voice. "Don't start the routine. Mr. Munn wants to talk to you."

"Talk to me?" I said, genuinely puzzled. "Listen, I didn't do anything to him."

Ignoring me, the principal pointed to his office and said, "He's in there waiting to see you."

Entering the inner office, I was even more impressed by being up close to this man. One glance at that tailored suit told me that people around my town didn't dress like that. Immediately I started to apologize for whatever it was that had happened to him and to assure him I didn't know anything about it.

With an overwhelming sense of warmth he shook my hand and told me he wanted to get to know me better. He drew a chair up close to mine and began to talk to me about myself. No one had ever said the things that he began to tell me.

YOU ARE DIFFERENT

Perhaps Melvin Munn went around the United States picking out the sorriest kid in the audience and working on him after the meeting. Possibly this afternoon was a unique experience for him, too. Whatever the reason, he was telling me that out of the whole audience he had noticed *me*. He had seen something special in me and felt it indicated a significant potential. Mr. Munn wanted me to believe that my life was very important and that I had talents that could be used in some unique way. As I listened I was transfixed by the whole conversation.

And then he said the words that went right to the heart of my whole being. "Robert, you are *different*, and that difference is a tremendous asset."

Beyond that point I don't have any idea what he said or how long the conversation lasted. Time froze for me around that sentence. I couldn't describe what was happening in my head, but I knew a new thing was taking shape. Something within me was being yanked up by the roots, pruned of the twisted, distorted limbs, and replanted in a new and fertile soil.

Melvin Munn had pulled up my implicit identity and recast it in a new form. Yes, I was different, but now I could call it good! I had a new image stamped on me, and it meant I really was somebody; I was going somewhere. Regardless of the past and the lack of achievement, a new door had been opened to the future. I could rejoice and believe that being different was a gift.

The next fall I enrolled in college. As I stepped from one world into a completely new environment, the difference was more than geography and educational level. I knew explicitly that I was different, and this time it felt good. Consequently, the results at the university were very good.

A TICKET TO SOMEWHERE

Unfortunately, not many of us have a Melvin Munn experience. Most of us have to find our own way out of the distortions that hold us captive. We need some help to see what we have been implicitly believing about ourselves. Moreover, we need guidance in learning how to establish an explicit identity that can become a new power in our life and our ticket to a better future.

The first step begins when we start to understand the implicit identity with which we have been living most of our lives. We need to dig down and get a firm grip on the definitions that have shaped our convictions about who we are. We have been building a life on either a positive or a negative basis. Either way, it is crucial that we uncover the guidelines that have directed our unconscious planning.

Initially, our unrevealed sense of identity may seem to be hidden in a place impossible to locate. Often we feel as if we are fishing in the dark with an unbaited hook in an unseen lake. We sense that there is something lurking just behind our thoughts, but we have no idea where the door to our mental backroom is located.

You can begin to fathom the unknown when you start to sensitize yourself to the clues that are scattered around your thinking. As you pick up on the subtle hints to your identity that are a part of your ideas and feelings, they will turn into road markers that can direct you to your personal information file which you have stored in your head.

I have found several questions that help me get personal clarification about how I really see myself. Let me suggest that you ask yourself these questions in a very slow and easy way. Take them one at a time and think through one answer before you go on to the next question. In fact, if it takes you several hours to finish reading the rest of this chapter, the time will be well spent. You are not trying to make a good grade on a test but are trying to be a Sherlock Holmes solving your own personal mystery.

Who is your hero? And why?

Sit back and ponder what person has been a guiding light for you. Perhaps the hero comes out of your childhood. It is quite possible that you may have changed heroes later in your life. Sometimes there are several people who together form a composite hero type for us.

But I want you to try to isolate the key person or persons who best personify your dreams. Once you have the name and face in mind, I want you to probe as many aspects and dimensions of the individual's personality as possible. Ask yourself exactly what is it that you like best about your hero. What do you see in this hero that you admire so much?

Then ask yourself why you feel so strongly about this hero. Why do you think this personal hero's traits are so significant to you?

When you have exhausted that question, begin to consider what this person or persons and these qualities tell you about yourself.

What you are doing is picking up one thread here and another thread there. But as you begin to pull on them, some will begin to get larger and larger. They will turn to string and hopefully to rope. When you pull the rope out, you may just find a big hunk of your identity tied to the other end.

What do you want most? And what will it get you?

Now shift gears and look in a slightly different direction. If any wish might be granted you, what would you ask for? Try to narrow your many requests and boil your wants down into one final "want." Again, you may find that you cannot settle on one item. In that case, list in order of preference what two or three wishes you would seek.

Think about your fantasies. When you are daydreaming, what do you seem to make come true? Those mental adventures are filled with clues about what you unconsciously desire the most.

After you have come to some conclusions, start looking between the lines. If that dream were to be fulfilled, what would it accomplish for you? What personal satisfaction or need would be filled? What need would be completed in your life?

As you begin to identify the needs that your wants and wishes represent, you will be really close to paydirt. Begin to push yourself harder. Why do I have that need in my life? Where does it come from? What bearing does a particular need have on the way I behave?

I find it very important to make notes when I am thinking about the black underside of my thoughts. Our best insights are very elusive and slip away from us. Like mercury, we find that identity clues slide through our fingers and cannot be held onto for very long. Our self-discovery may come in one shape and then quickly merge into another form that we didn't expect. However, if we have made some notation about our insights, we can make our minds stay on the track once the right direction is discovered.

What do you fear most? And why?
This question will be tricky. Often we can quickly identify a relatively superficial problem or situation which we would not want to happen. For example, I may be afraid of snakes or large dogs. Perhaps you would have a fear of an airplane crash or the traffic on the freeway. But don't let yourself settle for an obvious answer.

Beyond the surface desire to avoid pain or displeasure, what do you really dread? What would be the humiliation from which you would have a very hard time recovering?

For example, I find that I have two major fears that have deeply concerned me. The fear of failure and of being betrayed by someone I love are haunting deeply threatening. It took me a great deal of time to locate those sources of anxiety. But they are examples of what you might need to look for.

Once you have some concrete notes on your fear, begin to ask the "why" questions once more. What do these fears mean? What is the origin of your dread? How might you have constructed your life and relationships to protect yourself? What identity clues are hidden in your answers? If some of your answers surprise you, just keep pushing, because the implicit identity structures of our mind can be very cleverly disguised.

By this time you should have accumulated quite a bit of information about yourself. Most of what you have discovered will still be superficial, but if you have picked up the right threads you will be very close to making permanent and significant discoveries about why you act as you do. For long-term results you need to write this material down, so that you can go back and keep inquiring about its meaning.

BEGIN A JOURNAL

I urge you to begin a personal journal. This book will become the most confidential, secret diary of your soul. As you discover important personal insights, you will quickly write down your revelation.

In addition, as past incidents surface, be sure to describe what happened. Even more importantly, begin to decipher what these situations meant to you and what impact they have for your self-understanding. With time, you will find your implicit identity unfolding before your eyes like a spring plant coming into full bloom.

These three questions will help you to see your "idealized self." You can begin to understand who you would like to think you are. More importantly, you will start to know the implicit basis for your decisions. Don't worry if you don't like what you see. The negative can be turned into the positive once it is really clarified. But first you have to be ruthlessly honest.

Having kept a journal for a number of years, I have discovered a bonus: at one point in your life you will see one aspect of what your experience means. Yet when you reread that section a year, two years, or five years later, a much larger and unexpected picture will appear. In those moments of insight you can see the forces that have shaped and molded your very being. At those times you can have a most satisfying and deeply moving discovery. Rather than your life being a pawn in a game played by other people, you will know that you now have genuine control over your own future. You will have found the freedom to be a truly authentic person!

Moreover, you will be surprised at the incredible part Providence has played in the development of your personal history. What seemed to be fate is now clarified as a grand design that was at work, even though you didn't know anything about it. Chance will be unmasked and order revealed. Grace, the unmerited gift of life, was at work when you may have thought that only disaster and failure were to be the outcome of a long-past situation.

Once you see the order that has been working beneath the disorder in your life, you will have found your ticket to somewhere. From that point forward, no amount of disorder, either within or without, can undermine your personal stability. You will know that you have a destiny.

While you are probing for your own sense of order and design, you can also begin to take advantage of what an explicit sense of identity will do for you. Possibly by now you have some fairly good ideas about yourself. Therefore you need to take this implicit identity and very carefully scrutinize its implications. Just as my experience with Melvin Munn recast my self-understanding in a new form, you can do the same thing.

THE NEW FUTURE

When you take the implications of the Image of God as the new definitions of who you are, you will have found the building blocks for creating a new image. As your heroes, wants, and fears have previously shaped your life, so a similar set of values can have the same results.

I have found an exercise that has helped people in putting these new shapes together. It begins by describing what one's personal qualities can be if he chooses to accept the Imago as the source of his identity. Take a piece of paper and begin to write a list of adjectives that would be true of anyone who lived with such a model.

You might want to go back and consider what the last two chapters said about the Image of God. In addition, since Jesus Christ came in the fullness of that Image, you might try to describe what was exemplified in His life. For example, on my list I noted qualities like: significant, loved, valuable, capable, creative, worthwhile, etc.

Now I suggest that you take another piece of paper and draw a dividing line down the middle. At the top of one side put the heading "My Implicit Identity." On the other side write "My Explicit Identity—The Imago." Next, list in each column what you have discovered is true about each category. Once the list is complete, sit back to ponder the result.

Do you carry inside you the same identity that has been given you in God's sight? Is there a conflict between the negative ways that you see yourself and the very positive ways that God has intended you to be? How have you misjudged who you really are?

After a time of careful thought, I suggest that you

write out a paragraph on the theme "My True Identity."

In a few short sentences, describe who you really are and intend to be from that time forward. As you are writing, commit yourself to everything you are describing as being the complete and final truth by which you live from that moment forward.

When this project is done, begin to live daily with this new definition constantly in front of you. If you will make a number of copies, they can be put on the mirror in the bathroom, on the dashboard in your car, on your desk at the office, or any place where a reminder will have value.

In addition, I urge that you make this new definition the subject matter of a daily meditation. Set aside some time and place where you cannot be interrupted. Take your paragraph and cross out the places where you have used the personal pronoun "I" and write in "you." For example, you might have written, "I am a person who is loved in spite of any mistakes I have ever made and I am very valuable." Now it would read, "You are a person who is loved in spite of any mistakes you have ever made and you are very valuable."

In these quiet moments I want you to ask God the heavenly Father to begin to impress this new truth deep in your unconscious as well as conscious mind. Then begin to read the paragraph as if He is in fact speaking these very words to you. Silently let the meaning and message sink in. End this time by simply saying, "Thank You that You have made me who I am."

Once you are able to genuinely say "thank you," you will have established an internal gyroscope that cannot be thwarted by the time or the seasons. In an unstable world, you will have gained personal stability.

SUMMARY

Martin's Mental Health/Mental Illness survey suggests that the average American community has 600 schizophrenics, nearly 4000 alcoholics, 400 mentally ill children, 3000 homosexuals, and an incalcuable number of people suffering from depression. No one has statistics on the drug users and those who have "gone bananas"!

Here are seven principles that will help keep you from becoming a statistic.

1. *Get committed and quit being indifferent.*
Find out what is worthy of your energy and life; then take the plunge.

2. *Discover the source of stability.*
The key to reality lies in looking at life through the eyes of Someone who can distinguish between truth and the illusion. Jesus Christ is that Person.

3. *Integrity insures stability.*
Build your life on goals, commitments, and values that will last.

4. *Recover your inner center of strength.*
Build quiet pockets into your life. Retreat from the noise and pressure.

5. *Return to the original blueprints.*
Establish the Image of God as the reference point for your self-understanding. Refuse to accept personal definitions that are not in agreement with how God intended you to be.

6. *Construction is hard work.*
Discipline is an absolute necessity to forge and release the real you.

7. *Expect to build a new tomorrow.*
If you will pay the price for true self-discovery, you can expect to see a new person emerge. But don't wait for tomorrow! Get going today.

Part III

Keeping All Your Marbles In The Sack

A Concluding Grasp For Sanity

A Crazy Little Conversation With Margaret

Before I had time to acknowledge the phone call, the voice at the other end began to frantically inquire about whether I had heard a tape recording that seemed to be making the rounds of church groups.

"Listen, have you heard the things that this John Todd is saying? Do you realize he is a converted witch who knows the inside story on how the occult is getting ready to take over the world?"

"Well," I paused trying to let a sense of calm influence the conversation. "I have listened to his rather bizarre allegations."

"Well, they are startling!" Her reply obviously ignored my tone. "For example, he knows for a fact that President Carter is the Anti-Christ and Ruth Carter Stapleton is a high priestess of witchcraft." Her tempo increased with the next revelation, "And between Carter, the Rockefellers, Rothchilds' and the National Council of Churches, the whole world is going to be plunged into revolution!"

"Frankly, Margaret," I said, "I'm not sure

whether the man is giving a serious talk or is just a low grade commedienne trying out some new jokes."

"You can't be serious!" she exclaimed, shocked by my evaluation. "He absolutely documents that the Jewish Rothchild's are financing the take over." With an air of suspicion she continued, "Didn't you hear him say that many famous preachers are getting tens of thousands of dollars in pay-offs to keep their mouths shut?"

Now I decided to be a bit emphatic. "Margaret, this man proves nothing by documentation. In fact, he is a mass of contradictions and utter inaccuracies, blended together with a distinct flavor of anti-semitism and extreme right wing politics. How can you take such wild allegations seriously?"

Pausing for a slight moment she continued, "I just feel that in my heart all this is true. I just have a premonition about it."

Having caught her breath she was ready to convince me once more. "Because all these accusations sound so unbelievable, I know they are true. His ideas are so wild that they make sense out of the weird things happening everywhere."

"Now Margaret," I responded, "isn't craziness a rather poor criteria for judging sanity?"

"Oh no," she replied, "this man's allegations and ideas aren't any crazier than my everyday life. Anymore, I can believe just about anything."

I though to myself, "Yes, that really is a problem."

7

The Steeple
Over the Cuckoo's Nest

As I best recall, Jane and Bob had always been involved in church work. Since I hadn't seen them for several years, I was catching up on what had transpired in their lives since we were last together. So I inquired about what church they were attending.

"Oh, we don't go anymore," Jane replied cooly. "We have given up on it."

Remembering the extent of their past concern for religious things, I was taken back. "What happened?" I asked.

"Well," said Jane, "I've got enough problems as it is coping with life and staying sane without intentionally running around with people who are really crazy."

As our conversation continued, what had at first appeared to be iconoclastic began to clarify itself as a statement of simple fact. Jane had discovered a very important insight: many flipped-out people have run for refuge in the sanctuaries of American churches. Moreover, in far too many instances, weird things happening in religious guise have threatened to make some church groups appear more like mental institutions. And even worse, some religious groups that have fed off the current instabilities in American life seem to be feeding nuttiness right back into the lives of their converts. The end result is that the bizarre appears to be flourishing and multiplying in the name of divinity.

While I felt defensive and wanted to argue the point, actually I could remember a host of examples which substantiated Jane's reasoning. I've known some really crazy religious people.

Jane had made more than a casual observation about what had happened too often across the American religious scene. She was recognizing the amazing way in which people can talk themselves into endless varieties of gyrations in order to twist religious ideas to meet self-serving ends. Inevitably, the result is compounded craziness.

MARY ANN

One of my favorite crazy stories concerns Mary Ann. She showed up at the church one evening and bounded into our congregation with a burst of religious zeal. During the following weeks she gathered around herself a group of followers who attested to her unique and special religious insights. However, I was bothered by strange inconsistencies and quirks that kept surfacing in her behavior.

Several months later I got a phone call from a worried member who was concerned that Mary Ann's "secret life" was going to have a disastrous effect on the lives of her friends. She knew for a fact that Mary Ann was in the midst of a torrid affair with a married state legislator. The whole mess was about to break in the papers and would really cast a bad light on those associated with Mary Ann's religious activities.

Being young and impetuous, I decided to have a little talk with our newest zealot and to confront her with the story. Off we went for lunch together and a little time of "sharing." With the finesse of a gorilla, I dropped the bomb.

"Tell me, Mary Ann, about this affair you're having with Senator Jones," I asked calmly while terror lurked in my heart.

Her eyes increased in size about threefold, and she dropped her fork on the floor. "Oh my G-o-d!" was the sum total of her response.

As the blood came back to her face, she reached for my hand. "You must understand," she began; "it's really all right. Each time, just before we get in bed, we say the Lord's Prayer together."

I had an idea that this sort of thing is exactly what Jane had in mind.

In these incidents and many more like them, we are not talking about people who have gone crazy in the old clinical sense of mental illness. None of these individuals was a candidate for a state hospital. Yet their behavior clearly indicates that their perspective was distorted and that they were in retreat from some aspect of reality.

So we are back to our original description and definition of people "gone bananas." While in many areas of their lives these people are still functioning quite well, they are nevertheless playing with less than the proverbial "full deck."

THE RELIGIOUS CRAZIES

Since I have been recommending religious answers to contemporary personal problems, I must be completely honest with you about the problem of the religious crazies. While I am totally committed to the solutions that have been suggested for individual problems of instability, I also recognize that incredible distortions of truth have been made in God's name.

In addition, the highly subjective nature of personal religious experience can certainly open the door to abuse and perversion. I would be the first to admit that some of the worst crimes against mankind have been committed with "divine sanction." It is extremely important that we are clear about the difference between spiritual illusion a solid truth. The problem has become even more complicated because of groups that have conducted a wholesale baptism of crazy ideas and have given weirdness their version of divine blessing.

The Moonies, Jonestown, meditation cults, etc. have all been headline stories during recent months. Esoteric cults and guru-type preachers have sprung up like mushrooms. (Note: mushrooms flourish best in the dark and out of a particularly odious soil.) There is always some group, somewhere, promoting something, promising some result, if you will only send some money!

For a diversion from reality, I occasionally watched one enterprising television preacher who claimed to have discovered the secret of how God "stayed young." One evening he came forth with a new revelation. He was personally and singularly in possession of the truth about flying saucers. They were indeed from outer space and were being flown by seraphim and cherubim. And these angels of God were flying back to earth because they were really hacked off with sinful humanity! However, a small contribution to the Reverend would assure you that the saucers wouldn't stop in your backyard!

Recently I received an amazing letter from an evangelist who sent me a little prayer cloth. The personalized form letter guaranteed that the cloth had already been prayed over, and all I needed to do was place it under my pillow and sleep on it. All that remained was for me to write on the enclosed card what I wanted God to give me. When I returned the card and the prayer cloth (and an appropriate donation), the evangelist would personally pray over the cloth again and the answer to my request was guaranteed!

THE NEW TWIST

Of course, there is nothing historically new about these problems. For centuries, groups have been climbing mountains to greet the second coming of Christ. Crusaders sailed forth in the name of the love of Jesus to kill the infidels and heretics. Religious stock schemes and financial promotions are not original with the twentieth century. Distorted, cunning, deceptive religious practices have been common for countless generations across the globe.

However, the new twist is the massive use of religious gimmickry and diluted promises to shore up the social and personal illusions with which millions of people live. Frightened people bring their crises and crazies to church and ask that these be honored with divine respectability.

Unfortunately, there are always enterprising clergy types around who are quite easily persuaded to perform the rituals. These groups develop unspoken, implicit, common agreements about what they will together call "the truth." These pacts become their mutual defense against the realities they want to ignore or deny. Together they develop their own "devil" in the shape of whatever they happen to fear the most. The "enemy out there" becomes a projection of their own insecurities and anxieties. Actually, such groups may have quite rapid growth when the surrounding society is embroiled in great instability.

In times of chaos and confusion, people tend to seek an outspoken authority figure which they can hide behind. If this person can assure the group that they will not have to think for themselves, they will grant him great power. In such times of instability, any leader who can keep people from having to make real decisions and who will offer them shelter from the awful abyss of uncertainty that opens before them will become loved and followed with a total religious devotion.

In short, that is how we turn churches into cuckoos' nests.

But the purpose of this description is not to disillusion you about the possibility of finding genuine help from real faith. These pages are written to bring you solutions that can bring lasting stability into your life. However, to get to the truth we must sort out fact from fantasy. Failure to do so can cause us to be seriously misled and even to slip into fanaticism.

THE FANATICS

A fanatic might be defined as someone who has lost sight of the goal and doubled his energy in trying to reach it. That's the process which makes cults tick. I use Emil Brunner's definition of a fanatic as being someone who has the Word but has lost the Spirit. He suggests that the person may have an idea which is basically true, but he or she has lost a correct perspective on what the thought means. I am writing to find genuine solutions that will lead to clearcut goals which can be held with balance. Otherwise, even the truth we do have will be of little value.

When groups of people practice blind self-deception, their meetings become modern versions of "The Emperor's New Clothes." They develop a collective consensus about reality even though they may individually have unexpressed doubts and reservations. Finally someone will call nakedness what it is, and the castle comes tumbling down.

This phenomenon is not limited to churches and religious groups. The same experience happens within encounter groups, pop psychologies, therapies, political parties, and countless varieties of organizations that try to help people stave off personal crises. Fads regularly sweep across the country based on some clever Pied Piper's call to a new form of personal salvation. Immediately, groupees trumpet that "The Answer" has now been found. A flurry of excitement surrounds frantic meetings of the true believers. Then, somewhere out on the edge, someone snickers about something and once again nakedness is exposed.

Therefore we must examine carefully what constitutes an authentic answer in any search for spiritual direction. Once a person has identified with a group that has a defective sense of reality, he will tend to be bent along the same lines as that organization. We need to be able to recognize how and what causes people to end up with a bad case of the religious crazies.

GOING NUTS AT CHURCH

Ken Husey can help us understand what goes on in crisis-adjustment groups that have lost their way. In his play and the movie version of *One Flew Over the Cuckoo's Nest*, Husey takes us inside everyday life in a mental institution. The central character, R.P. McMurphy, schemes until he is admitted as a patient as an alternative to spending time in prison. While feigning insanity, he settles into the routine of the institution.

However, McMurphy soon makes a startling discovery. The inmates are actually no crazier than the average citizen out walking the streets! What is being called crazy is simply a game the inmates play with their custodians and the larger social system. "Craziness" is a choice they have made in order to avoid some aspect of reality, pain, or responsibility they don't want to face. Even the therapy sessions are part of the fortress they have built to wall out what they choose not to face. Like a wagon train circling around to protect against attack, the patients help each other avoid dealing with pain, decision, rejection, or fear. McMurphy's real problems come when he tries to break up the game and convince his fellow inmates to face the truth. They are there to avoid reality—not face it.

While realizing how explosive it got when McMurphy blew the whistle on the retreat-from-reality game, I must suggest that, for identical reasons, steeples are erected over cuckoos' nests. A wagon-train mentality sets in, and the group develops a religious rationale for what it does not want to face. And thus we begin to grow bananas in the church foyer.

Three major reasons which cause spiritual fact to be turned into fantasy are the source of much of the confusion that can cause people to pervert what could otherwise be the most help to them. Each reason is a basic ingredient in a wagon-train mentality of retreat.

CAMOUFLAGED FEELINGS

First, hidden emotional needs can become detours which lead to blind alleys. Such are either conscious or unconscious attempts to fulfill a legitimate emotional need through an illegitimate means. A basic need such as acceptance, security, importance, personal worth, etc. becomes a camouflaged motivation for the individual's religious interest and concern. For example, we have the "humble" preacher who loves attention or the self-effacing church woman who actually loves to dominate every meeting, etc.

In one sense it is quite valid for the Christian faith to promise fulfillment of our essential human need for meaning, purpose, destiny, and personal worth. The problems begin when people purposefully ignore truth in order to trim God, church, clergy, and creed to fit the fulfillment of the individual's current impulses. Such an illegitimate use of the Christian faith has historically spawned the wildest of aberrations.

For example, Joanne really gave us fits with her visions. She was 17 and a member of the local youth group. However, during prayer times she specialized in seeing the incredible. One evening two boys rushed into my office with the story that while Joanne had been staring at the cross while praying, she suddenly screamed out in terror. She told the group she had just had a vision of blood running down the cross and onto the floor. The boys weren't sure whether they were in the presence of a saint or a sickey.

Actually, Joanne was unaware of a hidden emotional need. The girl had a strong need for attention and affirmation. Unfortunately, she didn't get much affection at home and had stumbled onto how to supply that need at church. By having "visions" she got the esteem she missed in her life. As we gave her love and communicated that she was worthy, she was able to give up the nonsense.

Sigmund Freud recognized this problem long ago. He

diagnosed neurosis as often being a caricature of religion. He saw much of religious experience as an attempt to placate fears, dreads, and anxieties.[1] Though he seemed threatening to many religious people, Freud actually did everyone an important favor. He confronted us with the fact that fake emotional religious manuevers may, for a limited time, appear to be comforting, but these smokescreens are finally counterproductive.

WARPED YARDSTICKS

McMurphy and his fellow patients in the Cuckoo's Nest would be quick to pick up on a second cause of subverting spiritual reality into psychological escape. *One's personal needs become the measure of truth.*

When our wants become the ultimate gauge of truth, it is an open invitation for self-deception. Our hopes, dreams, fears, and apprehensions can keep our vision from surveying all the facts that surround a given situation. Churches, religious groups, psychological methods, and personal adjustment schemes have also been guilty of this self-deceiving tendency.

George is an example of how a crooked tape measure measured incorrectly. His involvement with the church had helped him settle many of his problems and needs. Yet he and his wife had inflicted each other with such deep wounds for so many years that their marriage had been mutilated almost beyond recognition. So I wasn't surprised to hear that he was involved with another woman.

My conversation with George began as he was making a decision about taking his new girlfriend to Las Vegas for a weekend. I asked George, "Given the nature of Christian morality, how did you decide to go ahead with the trip?"

"Well, Robert," he said with a tone of genuine sincerity in his voice, "I really did pray about it. In fact, I came down by the lake and really asked God to show me the way."

"What specifically did you pray?" I asked.

"I told God that if I shouldn't do it, He had better give me a sign."

"Don't tell me," I broke in; "I'll bet nothing happened."

"Exactly," he said. "And since God didn't say no, I knew it would be all right."

"Interesting," I observed. "You expected that God would do something that would make you an exception to everything He has said and done for at least four thousand years, and that He would exclude you from the Ten Commandments."

"Gee," he said, "I really never thought of it that way."

Too often we don't want to see things in such a clear light when our needs are pressing in upon us. Instead, we tailor the truth to fit the moment. The result is delusion.

A new and novel twist to the problem of self-deception has become a recent fad on the religious scene called "Positive Confession." When you "positively confess" you insist that God is going to do whatever you want done. If someone is dying of cancer, they are "to confess" or insist out loud that this is not so. They believe that the result will be that God will be forced to heal them.

This kind of practice is not so much a statement of conviction about the power of God to intervene in our lives as it is an insistence that we can make Him do what we want done; personal need is applied as the total measure of truth, and God must follow suit. These people are trying to blackmail God into fulfilling their wants.

Perhaps the best comment on "confessing" came from Dr. Jim Tanner. Jim is a vibrant man of faith who lives his life with great integrity and consistency. While making a medical call he was in an auto accident which left him permanently crippled. As a faithful man, he has accepted the problem and turned it into an asset.

Yet his friends cannot deal with his wheelchair. They keep wanting him to "confess" what God must do to get him back on his feet. In response to the pressure, Jim said to me, "But if you confess a lie, does that make it true?"

Needless to say, Jim can tell the difference between his needs and reality. Unfortunately, too many other people can't.

MAKING GOD YOUR TWIN

Another source of confusion results from *trying to create God in our own image.* Rather than accepting the given biblical description of the character of God, we develop a subjective idea that suits us better.

Freud recognized how this problem works. Though he characterized all personal religion as stemming from the personal creation of a god who is essentially an exalted father figure, he recognized that people often shape gods in the form of their emotional needs. Freud observed that when people are threatened, infantile needs for protection come into play; individuals tend to seek powers beyond themselves to save them.

Not only individuals, but groups, ban together to develop a collective image of a god that will offer comfort for their mutual woes. If you spend enough time with these groups, you will soon be amazed at how much their god looks exactly like them. From such groups, cult leaders develop. These leaders take on the characteristics which the groups attribute to their local deity.

While the mass suicides at Jonestown are almost unparalleled in history, the principles at work are frighteningly predictable. Jim Jones became the embodiment of the fears, desperations, and hopes of a mass of socially disinherited people. It should be no surprise that hundreds of the bodies were never claimed. The creation of a god in the image of Jones proved to be monstrous.

Don't blame the Christian faith when people create a god which they describe with biblical words but which is essentially fashioned out of a mold of their own choosing. Actually, we are not so different from those ancient ancestors who had gods of fertility and power. Contemporary deities are still being cast in the form of race, class, patriotism, profit, youth, etc. Such confusion over the difference between what is *us* and what is truly *Him* cannot result in anything but emotional disorientation.

The inescapable fact is that in the beginning we were created in His image, and not the other way around. Consequently, there is an objective quality about His nature which doesn't change with the times or the seasons. As a result of the way He is, truth doesn't change. We are able to fly off into space, run computers, and calculate probabilities because He has created the universe with predictable boundaries and limits. We find freedom and stability, not by rearranging truth, but by living in harmony with the way He created things.

GETTING THE BATS OUT OF THE BELFRY

If we can keep from stepping in a cuckoo's nest we will be able to find the strength that spiritual reality promises. Saint Augustine taught that the closer one comes to truth, the closer he will come to God. I would suggest a corollary of that statement: the closer one comes to God, the closer he must come to truth. Genuine faith will always lead us to reality and personal integrity. Our quest is for such genuineness.

One obvious clue in finding the right path to lead us out of the woods is the integrity of any group or organization that is offering us guidance. Unless a church, society, movement, etc. has authenticity, we cannot expect personal progress. Learn to ask yourself questions about all schools of thought, psychological organizations, parachurch movements, etc.

Does the group have a history? Is there a basis for evaluating what they do? How long have they existed? Any group that cannot furnish credentials which can be examined ought to be suspect. The best guarantee of the validity of any church or clergyman is a long tradition of being a part of the established church.

Groups that have nothing to be afraid of will be open. You should be able to see data about finances and management. On the other hand, be wary of organizations that are centered around charismatic personalities who avoid questions about their operation. One-man shows tend to have poor track records.

The failure to check thoroughly into any organization that is going to influence your life is an open invitation to disaster. One of the terrible ironies of the Jonestown disaster is that a sign over Jim Jones' platform chair read, "Those who do not remember the past are condemned to repeat it."

In addition, how can we make sure we don't repeat the mistakes out of our own emotional history? We need to make sure that our own fears, anxieties, and dreads do not cause us to clutch desperately after any form of relief. Therefore, let's return to the question of identity which has been considered previously.

THE TRUE MIRROR

The people we have discussed in this chapter have a common problem. They are all victims of their impulses and they lack the internal strength to sort out right from wrong, appropriate from inappropriate. Such distorted perspective flows from one's lack of a sense of identity.

Previously, we have seen that the Image of God offers us a true mirror that reveals a reliable reflection of who we are. There is one further dimension of the Image that needs to be included to help us deal with our fears and misgivings.

The Image of God was demonstrated completely in

Jesus Christ. The way in which He appropriated His own enormous emotional strength and integrity from that sense of identity has important implications for us. His lifestyle reflected perfect balance and maturity. Those who identify with Christ find that they have discovered the secrets of how to fearlessly face the truth and reality of any situation they encounter.

What are those secrets?

First, you can confront what might otherwise be unspeakable terror. Through the victory of Christ over His cross, there is extended to you the same possibility to face any confrontation. You can face your own personal fears and conquer them.

The cross is a picture of a love that would not withdraw or recoil from dread and rejection. Because He had total confidence in God the Father's ability to vindicate the truth, Jesus could stand His ground when personal doubts and misgivings were pushing in upon Him. Moreover, the crucifixion is the story of how pain can capture victories that are unknown to those who live by taking the route of least resistance. On this basis you can know that your present trial may become your finest hour of self-discovery.

You can have hope by knowing that you do not have to enter such encounters by yourself. Having identified with the Christ, you have a hidden and guaranteed part in the way in which God was in Christ, overcoming the obstacles of life.

As the strength of God is added to your best efforts, you will be surprised to discover a vitality that you did not know existed. That energy is found *only* through the encounter with conflict.

THE NEW POSSIBILITIES

When you embrace what you fear in the name of Christ, that apprehension can and will undergo a special metamorphosis. Things which can't be changed can still be transformed. When you plunge into a situation you want to avoid, you will be surprised at the new possibilities which emerge before your eyes.

Francis of Assisi discovered this principle. While riding his horse across the Umbrian Plain, he came upon a leper huddled by the road in dirty rags. In Medieval society, these hideous beggars were to be avoided at all costs. Yet Francis was moved with compassion as he looked on the man's utterly abandoned condition. Something deep within Francis stirred him to embrace this woeful figure. In the name of Christ he bent down to comfort the diseased wretch.

To his astonishment, the leper became the Christ! The object of repulsion had turned into the source of love itself. Francis was later to realize that hidden in this story was a parable which is available for all of us. Facing one's anxieties in the name of Christ is the key that unlocks the doors which lead to a transformed tomorrow.

Even experiences that we have repressed will yield and dissolve themselves when the person begins to live out such an open style of life. Theologian Jurgen Moltmann suggests that our repressions "are done away with through sympathy and love, through the acceptance of what is otherwise unacceptable, through the ability to suffer, and through sensitiveness."[2] He is suggesting that even the fears from the past can be redeemed.

Many of us have hidden lepers of the heart that have lived within us for years. Our fear of facing these villains of the past have allowed them to roam unobstructed through the unconscious recesses of our minds. The time has come to discover that even those painful memories have the potential of having Christ living there in camouflaged form.

Everything in our past is usable to God. What is feared can be faced. What is faced can be embraced. And when the sores of yesterday are touched with the gentle kiss of Christ, even what is ugly gives way to becoming a new expression of beauty.

SUSAN

As you more completely take on a true sense of identity, these changes can happen to you. Perhaps you are wondering if identifying with Jesus Christ can really produce such emotional stability. Susan found that it certainly can.

During her adolescent development, Susan had looked for some strength and guidance through various religious practices. But as an adult she was challenged to find a new identity through Jesus Christ. Her new-found faith did not offer her a retreat from facing the truth about herself. The closer she came to God's reality, the more Susan was forced to face up to the facts about her life. Finally one afternoon she came to talk with me.

With tears in the corners of her eyes she began, "There are a number of things I must tell someone; but I'm afraid of what you will think of me if I level with you." I assured her of the confidential nature of any form of confessional conversation. We talked about how unburdening ourselves can have a cathartic effect.

"I feel that God is insisting that I face up to some things I've tried to hide from for many years," Susan continued. "I've got to get these things out of my mind."

Then Susan poured out an avalanche of experiences from her adolescent years. The feeling of not being loved by her parents had created hate and animosity for them. Her frustrations at home had led her into sexual adventures which had left her with haunting memories. As she related her story, her quiet sobbing painted its own picture of inner brokenness.

Then somewhere from beneath her tears new words began to take shape. "But now for the first time I feel like maybe I'm going to be free of all that. Not only can I believe I am forgiven, but I think I can forgive myself." Susan paused and then added, "Something died in me a long time ago, and I believe that today God has finally helped me bury it."

In other counseling sessions Susan continued to face herself honestly and to take on the new realities that the Image of God offered her. Slowly but clearly a new person began to emerge, and her life became marked by stability.

FOLLOWING THE YELLOW BRICK ROAD

In *The Wizard of Oz,* Dorothy was told that the yellow brick road would lead her out of her desperation and bring her the answers to all her fears. But the Wizard was a hoax and the road was only part of a fantasy.

Unfortunately, the world is filled with people who want a God that is like the Wizard was supposed to be. They look for churches, groups, and movements that will be their yellow brick road. In the end, they too are left with only their delusions as a reward for their efforts.

There is a moral to this story: the greater the potential for good, the greater the potential for perversion. Certainly that is true in the religious realm.

Our fantasies make a poor substitute for God's truth. Nevertheless, the religious failures and church crazies are still essentially testimonies to a real power that is available to all who will sort out the authentic from the phony, the honest from the deceptive.

This identity which is ours through the Image of God is a gauge by which we can measure the true and the false. On the basis of what has happened in Jesus Christ we do have an authentic guide to distinguish between what is crazy and what is sane.

People who are following the way of Christ don't need yellow brick roads.

---

1. J.E. Scharfenberg, *Sigmund Freud und Seine Religicon-skirth Als Herausforderung fur den Christenken Glauben,* 1968, i. p. 137-139.
2. Jurgen Moltmann, *The Crucified God* (New York: Harper and Row, 1974), p.16.

8

How to Stay Sane

Bob has always been one of these strong, stable people with whom I like to kick ideas around. His sense of bearing has helped me stabilize my own thoughts. I asked him how he kept so balanced in the midst of all the turmoil going on in the business world.

"Oh, I have no trouble staying sane," Bob replied. "I just change my definition of sanity whenever it's necessary."

Well, that's one way to assure yourself that you haven't gone crazy! Actually, a lot of people follow that practice. In fact, we keep inventing new words and phrases to reflect the constantly changing definition of sanity that is going on all around us.

Recently in *The New York Times Magazine*, William Safire traced the progression of "kook" and "Cuckoo" in the 1950's to "kooky" and "spaced out" in the 1960s. Today, as emotional imbalance is discussed, we seem to be settling on "flakiness" as our new noun or adjective or whatever.[1] The point is to keep our craziness socially respectable according to the current popular standards.

THE RADICAL SHIFTS

Following these social changes in what is currently considered sane or crazy is not easy. The shifts are more than just slightly radical! For example, for weeks the headlines told the story of Bill and Emily Harris, who, along with Patty Hearst, were holding up banks and stores. Their explanation for what they were doing was that as social revolutionaries they were making America a better place and eradicating evil from the streets.

In Chicago they have a new service called "Dial-A-Gasp." For 19 dollars a year a person can join and receive a special list of women who like to receive obscene phone calls. Women call into the service and leave their numbers. In turn, the agency is able to get the callers together in the privacy of their own homes.[2] What was once considered normal seems to have changed somewhat in Chicago!

In the scramble to find personal direction, people are grasping at every conceivable source for help. Regardless of the facts, people are giving credibility to a wide assortment of strange social aberrations. The newspaper columns with the predictions of Jeanne Dixon are an amazing example of this desperate search for direction. In 1978 she predicted:

> —*President Carter would be attacked by terrorists*
> —*Amy Carter would be a diplomat*
> —*The ancient culture of Tibet would be completely lost*
> —*A new war would start in Vietnam*
> —*Pope Paul would have amazing vigor*
> —*and more than a half-dozen other events that didn't happen.*[3]

Yet each day millions of readers look at her horoscope predictions as a sure-fire guard against the unseen pressures that may arise and drive them crazy before nightfall.

Ours has become the world of the bizarre and the confounding. In the Jonestown massacre, hundreds of people committed suicide for seemingly religious reasons. However, one explanation for their willingness to be led to death is that a high percentage of these people were from poverty-stricken backgrounds. Childhood deprivation had created a paranoia that made these people easy targets for manipulation.

On the other hand, we keep hearing more about the strange life of Howard Hughes. Though he was one of the world's wealthiest men, he lived in squalor and meager circumstances because he too was paranoid. With these stories as the backdrop to our everyday experience, it is more than a little difficult to judge what "normal" really means. In fact, as previously observed, "normal" doesn't seem to exist anymore.

WHAT IS SANITY?

To stay rational we need to have a definition of sanity which does not change. We will have problems knowing whether our perceptions of reality are valid unless we can grasp some objective idea of what is truly normal. To maintain a balanced emotional state we must have moorings that do not shift with the tides of social change.

In previous chapters we have discussed how "normal" has been lost through the radical and rapid shifts that have taken place in American life. In addition, we have also probed how an individual sense of identity has in many instances not given the internal gyroscope necessary for maintaining an inner orientation that is required for a sense of personal security.

The foregoing pages have also led us to the discovery that there is a basis on which we can establish our lives other than the basis given us by our confused society. That basis is rooted in the Person of God.

This is a quality given by God that is intended to be an intricate part of who we are and what we do. This God-basis can fill in the blank spaces in our existence and is also crucial for reestablishing the norms which are so vital for our emotional well-being. From this same source we can also develop a definition of sanity that will not change with the turning of the seasons.

In the last chapter I stated that the most complete expression of the fullness of the Image of God was demonstrated in the man Jesus of Nazareth. It follows that Jesus would also be an authentic model for what a sane person would be and do. From His life we should be able to deduct a definition of stability that can lead us through the modern morals of indecision.

Perhaps you are ready to accept this idea. Then again, maybe you're not. If not, before we can go any further together, you need to recognize the alternatives.

C.S. Lewis's impeccably logical mind developed the possible conclusions. He noted that people are quick to admit that Jesus was a great teacher or a great man without also believing that He was uniquely the Son of God and Messiah. He observed that the problem of this position is that Jesus claimed neither to be a great teacher nor a humanitarian. Rather, Jesus claimed and taught that He is the Christ and God in flesh. If this is not true, Jesus is hardly a great teacher or an extraordinary person. Rather, He was a liar or deranged. Lewis forces us to the conclusion that Jesus was either who He said He was or else He is not really worthy of our consideration at all.[4]

You already know my conclusion. The impact of His life on 20 centuries of history has been to lead people to truth and sanity. The historic exceptions to that path have always been demonstrable deviations from the norms that He established and taught. Therefore, I am personally quite ready to believe that Christ offers us a far better pattern for normality than anything which has ever been developed from academic and social institutions.

FIVE CHARACTERISTICS OF STABILITY AND SANITY

On that basis, I want to share with you five qualities which I have discovered in Christ's life. From these characteristics I believe we can develop a definition of sanity which will give us clear and strong personal direction. These five attributes are: perspective, balance, appropriateness, harmony, and actualization.

I find that the interaction of these characteristics produced the most stable life the world has ever observed. Once each word is defined, I believe we will be able to discover a definition of sanity that can give real guidance. In addition, discussing these qualities will help develop a more complete picture of what a sane and stable person can be.

PERSPECTIVE

Basically, mental illness is a loss of perspective. Whether the source is organic or functional, a person's inner orientation is gone and he has lost the ability to see himself in correct relationship to others, to his personal history, or to a proper course of action. The problem of "going bananas" is just one of degree. Though "being zonkers" is more temporary, the person has still lost the ability to see beyond his present confusing moment.

In contrast, one of the hallmarks of Jesus' life was His ability to bring issues into a new and fresh perspective. Old prejudices and fears were challenged by His particular view of what events and values should mean. He had the insight to put the present moment in its proper tension with the past and the future. From His teachings and actions we can get an idea about what perspective means.[5]

Perspective causes us to consider our emotional needs in the light of their effect on others. If our wants are destructive, then perspective demands retreat and reconsideration. Moreover, manipulative ploys that diminish and impune others can't be considered valid. Perspective requires reflection on what is best for all concerned.

Perspective can change immobilizing emotions into the raw material of courage and fortitude. When Great Britain was faced with impending national disaster as Hitler began aerial bombing attacks, Winston

Churchill called the nation together by asking them to make constructive use of their fear. He suggested that they respond with such "blood, sweat, and tears" that though the empire lasted for a thousand years, their time would be remembered as "our finest hour." Many Englishmen found new stability through that perspective.

In addition, perspective helps us resist the tyranny of urgent pressures that would blind us from seeing how ideas or actions need to be set in the framework of history. We constantly are asked to "do it now" and not be concerned for the future. Perspective requires that I remember that there was always a yesterday and there will still be a tomorrow. Moreover, perspective means that we learn not to take ourselves too seriously. None of us is going to get out of this world alive anyway, so a little sense of humor about our fallibility and limitations helps a great deal.

Asking ourselves key questions can help put a situation back into proper focus. One of Jesus' techniques in teaching was to ask questions of His hearers. He asked such questions as: Am I considering all the factors that have influence on my situation? If not, why am I resisting certain issues? Or try this question: If I project myself five years into the future, what would I think about my present course of action? If I discussed this problem with Jesus of Nazareth, what might He say about the issues? Such questions help put rationality back into emotionally charged situations.

BALANCE

Now let's move to a second characteristic that marked the life of Jesus. While moving through both physical and emotional storms of hurricane proportion, He maintained an amazing sense of composure. While others retreated in terror, Jesus reflected such a sense of balance that He was recognized clearly as being the master of the situation at hand.

Balance can be described as emotional equilibrium. It is the ability to hold opposing emotional forces and stresses in constructive tension. Balance is the emotion-juggling act that keeps us from becoming captive of one particular feeling during a period of stress.

Balance is a quality that enables us to recognize that many forces come to bear on every feeling, wish, or decision.

Being able to be aware of those factors and to recognize their significance is the hallmark of a balanced person. Another aspect of such equilibrium is the ability to live comfortably with the paradoxical. So often the forces that bear down upon us seem to be in total opposition to each other, while at the same time they are all completely valid. A balanced person is able to handle these ironies of life.

A lack of balance affects our perception of events much as physical distortion determines what we can see. When the eye has problems, the physical images are fuzzy and blurred. In the same way, emotional balance either does or does not give us clear images of what is happening to us.

For example, many people are bothered with one of three common problems: myopia, hypermetropia, and astigmatism. Myopia means that we cannot see objects in the distance as well as we can see what is immediately in front of us. Far-off things appear blurry and undefined. On the other hand, hypermetropia is just the opposite: the horizon line may seem very clear, but the page before us is unintelligible. Finally, astigmatism is a distortion of the shape of the eyeball which creates images that are out-of-focus and may see to be double. Consequently, glasses are required to restore balanced vision.

Often we "go bananas" for very similar reasons. Our emotional balance has a corresponding malfunction that keeps feeding us perceptions that are inaccurate. For example, being emotionally myopic is common in many religious groups. They are experts on what is under their noses but have no feel whatsoever for the larger horizons of the world outside. While they feel the urgency of their immediate personal concerns, they lack an emotional grasp of the issues that encompass something larger than their own navels.

On the other hand, hypermetropia, or farsightedness, is a problem that is more common on college campuses, in the human potential movements, and with radical women's libbers. While being concerned with their emotional needs, their vision is so focused on the lofty goals of the future that they may totally misread the emotional context in which they are living. Thus we get the woman who is passionately concerned with her career while having no perception of what is going on in the lives of her children or her husband. Or there is the type of man who has strong and forceful feelings about the misuse of nuclear energy and environmental pollution but who cannot maintain an adequate on-going personal relationship on a one-to-one basis.

Finally, emotional astigmatism can be described as a problem of always "feeling double." Such people tend to read hidden "other" connotations into what they hear and experience. Usually the result is that they feel victimized or "used" by those around them. At the least, they feel unsure and unclear about what their experiences really mean.

Such a loss of balance causes people to read more into a situation than is really there. For example, I once worked with a woman who was constantly changing her telephone number and mailing address. In addition, she kept large quantities of food hidden in case of an overnight collapse of the economy. She would interpret the most casual contacts as having the potential of concealing constant surveillance. Double meanings were hidden everywhere!

Once again, asking ourselves questions can help to reestablish balance. In fact, the right questions can have the same effect as glasses do for the eyes. For example, equilibrium is often restored by asking, "What makes me feel so strongly about this issue?" or "What need in my life does this issue really represent?" Another question might be, "Since nobody is 100 percent right or 100 percent wrong, what are some possible ways in which I might be wrong?" or "Where could I not be completely right?" Insight always comes when one considers what need the other person may have operating in any conflict or encounter.

The point is that balance is crucial for emotional stability. It requires the ability to correctly perceive the nature of the forces and factors pushing in upon us and in turn to be able to make authentic and adequate responses to these pressures. Balance is absolutely necessary for personal solidarity.

APPROPRIATENESS

At this point you might want to raise an objection. Perhaps the type of adjustment that has been described so far could be interpreted as an accommodation to the status quo. Someone might charge that I am merely describing an adaptation to some form of middle-class-mindedness in which we learn to smile in all directions and resolve any tension at all costs. It is particularly at this point that envisioning Jesus Christ as the ultimate model of stability makes a radical difference, for His sense and expressions of appropriateness were anything but accommodation.

A quick consideration of the meaning of appropriateness tells us that is a quality which is generally relative to something else. Appropriateness is determined by values which we bring to a particular situation. For example, it is acceptable to tell jokes at a party but not at a funeral service. It is okay to tell my son that his clothes look terrible and the colors clash, but the same message will not be received well by the checker at the supermarket.

Our problem is to figure out what it is that makes for appropriateness, and this is not always clear. For example, many mentally ill people feel they are being completely appropriate in terms of what they believe is true. In Peter Barnes' play *The Ruling Class*, we are introduced to Jack the Earl of Guerney. While Jack is a nobleman of the English aristocracy, he is also a paranoid schizophrenic who believes himself to be Jesus Christ. He finds it completely appropriate to expect people to address him as "Holiness" and "Son of God." However, his expectations lead him to being institutionalized. The better "something else" has obviously eluded him.

Contemporary society with the "bananas" problem is caught in a relatively similar bind. Too often our reference points have been developed out of our social delusions. In turn, we are not sure what really does fit well. So, rather than living by a chosen sense of style, we respond to fads. We get such phenomona as 18-year-olds' stretch pants on 50-year-old bottoms; middle-aged men emulating teenagers; and children whose ideas of reality are shaped by violence, sex, and superficiality on TV. Though we may not be as crazy as the Earl of Guerney, some of our expectations are not much better.

At this point the sanity of Jesus is most helpful. But it requires a careful examination because often His responses were not what was expected. When faced with people whom the society thought He ought to condemn, He responded with forgiveness. When seemingly rational people were in retreat, He charged forward. Rather than being bound by many of the prevailing social conventions of His day, He exhibited a complete freedom to seek a different direction. In the midst of His variations, He still moved according to an absolute code that imparted to Him a quality of appropriateness that has transcended the centuries. Our question must be: What was that code? What was His particular system?

He called it the kingdom of God. Space doesn't allow

an elaboration of the massive theology involved in that idea, but we can get a condensation of these themes in the Sermon on the Mount. Studying that section of Matthew's Gospel and then reflecting on how Jesus lived that message can give us a picture of where His responses originated.

Behind His actions was a God-based morality that stood in contrast to the ideas of His time. His own personal dignity was grounded in the Image of God. Such a sense of dignity automatically dictated what did and did not fit. Moreover, out of His personal relationship with God the Father came His particular sense of personal destiny. Therefore, whatever the situation was, whatever was happening in His personal encounters, His response came forth in light of these "givens." This was the secret of His appropriateness.

The difference between politicians and statesmen is that statesmen live by their code. In contrast, the actions of politicians are generally based on what is expedient. There is a similar disparity between what makes most people common and a few uncommon. The same contrast has deeply significant implications for our stability.

Our actions need to spring from an inner reservoir fed by the overflow from a carefully considered value system. When our responses are based on the same source of ethics, morality, personal dignity, and destiny as seen in Jesus, then a natural sense of appropriateness will follow. Such naturalness is one of the hallmarks of the stable person.

HARMONY

Now let's explore how the meaning of harmony was manifest in the life of Jesus. He has more unique class for us to use in making our pilgrimage toward wholeness.

Harmony is a big idea. It involves peace of mind, but is a much larger concept. We can have a certain kind of peace of mind about our actions or decisions and still not have an abiding sense of harmony. On the other hand, harmony encompasses peace of mind in such a way that, once acquired, we also have a true and enduring mental tranquility.

The kind of harmony we find in Jesus essentially contains three ingredients. The first two characteristics are amity within ourselves and with others. We come to an internal and external conciliation in our relationships. The third element is a sense of fraternity with the universe. There is a deep sense of knowing that we have found our proper place in the scheme of things. These three elements combine to impart an abiding sense of well-being that continues even while the storms of life rage.

Jesus demonstrated such a constant harmony and displayed it in so many unexpected circumstances that this characteristic is one of the most obvious qualities of His ministry. He was never a man divided against Himself. In fact, during times of extreme conflict He was able to wrestle with issues until they were resolved in a way that was consistent with His identity. He could then proceed with enormous personal unity. Jesus' emotional struggle with His future in the Garden of Gethsemane is such an incident.

His relationships with people were so positive that multitudes were magnetically drawn to Him. Yet the most dramatic illustration of His accord with others was the manner in which He dealt with His enemies. The ability to say "forgive them, for they know not what they do" demonstrates a harmony of the most profound depth.

Less obvious, but equally important, was the harmonious interplay He had with nature. His own profound sense of being at peace with the universe is displayed in the illustrations in which He used flowers, animals, clouds, etc. as metaphors to teach higher truth. When confronted by illness, he bestowed health. Even the sudden storms that turned the Sea of Galilee into thundering waves were stilled by the unique words of harmony He spoke to them.

Clearly, anyone who can master a similar variety of harmony will have achieved genuine stability. He or she will be equipped to stay sane even when surrounded by maddening circumstances. Unfortunately, only a minority of modern people have acquired this gift.

Since the Enlightenment, the advent of science, and the industrial revolution, Western man has had a difficult time finding a peaceful place in his world. Our own time has witnessed the violent reaction of many people against the circumstances that society had given them. The youth rebellion of the sixties was in many instances a reaction against the artificiality of the ideals and values of their parents. Many collegiates found that they had a deep hunger for a "more natural" way of life than they had grown up with.

The impersonal city, endless concrete roads, and freeways that constantly spawn more and more cars have not lent themselves to the establishment of a sense that all is well in the world. The pollution of the air and the ground has left us troubled and uneasy about the future.

The current social philosophies of hedonism and selfishness have essentially separated people and left us divided against ourselves. Many people who have successfully sought after a better emotional adjustment to the past are still left without any experience of true harmony. In the last part of this chapter I will discuss how this harmony can be acquired.

ACTUALIZATION

The last characteristic to be considered is just as vital and necessary as the other four. Actualization is the quality that enables us to turn all the other attributes of stability into performance.

Actualization is defined as the ability to "realize in action or fact."[6] Essentially, this quality is necessary for turning our ideas, decisions, and dreams into results. We are moved from contemplation to the concrete application of our thoughts.

Often the contemporary literature on successful personal adjustment overlooks this capacity. Often the description of emotional stability turns out to be a form of stoic resignation to accept the "inevitables" and to passively go on one's way. The world is left no better than it was found—perhaps a little worse. The important thing is to "feel happy," whether it makes any difference or not.

Some forms of mental illness, such as schizophrenia with delusions of grandeur, are particularly marked by expectations that can never find realization. Though not as obvious, instability often reflects itself in endless conversations about what one is going to do but which never happens that way. A prize example is the soap operas. On any given afternoon, we get endless conversations about what Vanessa will do if Rod does something rash which depends on how Heather feels about Bruce's decision to respond to Nicole's advances conditioned by Melvin's fears about . . . and so forth. Most of the "soaps" are actualization running in reverse.

Such forms of indecision do not make for personal stability. In addition, the inability to act on what we feel ought to be done only contributes more frustration to our problems. When we are finally able to acquiesce only to the status quo, we are not demonstrating strength but rather cowardice.

In complete contrast, the life of Jesus was marked by action. He so completely embodies what He thought and believed that it is not possible to separate His ideas from His performance. Jesus' personal unity between the thought and its expression marked His life as being a complete example of actualization. Consequently, a hallmark of those who have understood and followed Him has been that they left their world a different and better place than they found it.

Actually, there is a very important principle of mental health operating behind this quality. William James, the great psychologist, recognized that our actions shape and develop our attitudes. Often we believe that our feelings are the basis for our actions, but James noted that how we act can actually determine our emotions. People who are actualizing their ideas can be creating new feelings of confidence and well-being.

For example, we may be afraid of entering a dark building even though we know that there is nothing inside that can harm us. Once we have demonstrated boldness by entering the blackness and finding the light switch, we truly begin to feel courageous and brave. Another example is the Dale Carnegie Course's method of teaching people to stand in front of a mirror and say, "Act enthusiastic and you will be enthusiastic." As that is done with forceful body actions, a new and genuine enthusiasm begins to surge through the individual. Actualization creates its own special climate of personal satisfaction.

Stability requires the ability to act. Personal wholeness demands that we are able to realize what we have conceived to be important. The closer we come to a complete unity between what we think and do, the greater will be our proximity to sanity.

A DEFINITION FOR UNDEFINED TIMES

Now we are in a position to find the definition of rationality that we need. By compiling these qualities into a single statement, we ought to have an answer that is more permanent than the usual ideas blowing in the prevailing social wind.

Sanity is a balanced state of mind manifesting perspective and harmony which enables the individual to both act and to react in appropriate ways.

Now we have a path we can follow. This definition can help us in a number of ways when we feel we are on the verge of flipping out. Since we have explored its terms, we now have at least five road signs to point the way.

In my experience, I find that people tend to naturally have certain strengths and weaknesses in these five areas. One individual may tend to see things with good perspective but lack the appropriateness necessary to express his or her insights well. Other persons may manifest a strong degree of harmony in all their relationships, but they never get anything done. Their good intentions never find adequate expression.

By carefully analyzing your thoughts, relationships, decisions, etc., you can find clues to the areas in which you are limited. Using these five characteristics as your measuring stick, try to discover which areas are your strengths and where you are the weakest. When you have an idea where your blind side is, you'll know where to start seeking help when life begins to overwhelm you. You'll have new clues to the problems when you begin feeling a little irrational or disoriented.

We go bananas when one or two of these components of sanity are temporarily not functioning. If more than two areas are not working, we are likely to be momentarily immobilized. The most serious mental and behavioral disorders develop when we have lost control of two or more components for an extended period of time. When the possibility of loss appears to be possibly permanent, we must begin to consider institutional care.

These five elements in a definition of sanity offer concrete guidance in the search for stability. We can consider these qualities as norms and moorings to which we can anchor. When surrounded by people who don't know where they are going, we have found definite direction.

KEEPING YOUR HEAD SCREWED ON

All of us *do* want to be people who know what's happening. We hunger to be on top of life and to be adequate. In these final pages I want to share a very practical method which will help you use the ideas that have been discussed throughout this book.

The cultivation of the five characteristics of stability and sanity will build new strength into your emotional life, but unless you take specific steps to make this happen, the ideas will do nothing for you.

Begin by practicing a discipline that helps work all these characteristics into your life. Learn to keep yourself centered. Once you develop the habit of "centering," you will be on your way to implementing these ideas that are critical for lasting change.

I stumbled onto the meaning of centering while studying sculpture and ceramics and learning to use a potter's wheel. The wet lump of clay and the whirling disk began preaching their own sermon to me. They spoke well. I dropped a lump of clay onto the center of the wheel. Carefully I began to use my hands to shape the clay into a round, cone-shaped mound. The force of the spinning wheel caused the clay to take on a perfectly formed, cylindrical roundness. Slowly and cautiously I placed my thumbs in the center of the mound and started opening the ball so that a shape could develop.

But unless the clay is perfectly centered on the wheel, the weight will not be distributed correctly when the ball is opened. The result is that the walls of the clay object are uneven, and soon the cylinder rising off the wheel becomes whobbly and caves in. Unless the clay is centered, nothing stable can be built.

As the wheel was spinning, I was struck by how much my emotional life was like the process going in beneath my hands. Everything depended on how well-centered I was—emotionally and spiritually. When I was sloppy and off-target, the result would be a life that is like a bent and distorted pot. I had to pull all the emotions, ideas, dreams, needs, and relationships that churned inside me together as they revolved around a center. Correct proportioning and harmonizing of all these factors was critical so that they would move in the same direction from the center. Once centered, the harmony and balance imparted to my life would automatically solve many problems.

Later I was to discover that centering requires that I line up the core of my personality so that it comes to center in a relationship with God. I get in touch with the "Me" that lives at the focal point of my experience of life, and I align that with God as I best understand Him. Rather than being pulled in many directions, I settle in on what it means to be me in light of who He is. That source of identity becomes the perfect target for the rest of my centering.

As my life goes whirling on its way, I resolve to bring its many components into a creative and balanced tension with the one center. I use the five characteristics of sanity and stability as measuring sticks to test whether I am valid or invalid in what I am thinking and doing. Each aspect is measured against a God-based morality. From my relationship with Him I can gauge whether decisions are or are not in accord with the destiny I should be pursuing. Obviously, this whole process produces harmony and a deep sense of well-being.

You will need three tools to sculpture your life. First, you need to keep a journal of your spiritual and emotional pilgrimage. Each day, or at significant moments, record what is happening and how you feel about the event. You may want to philosophize a bit about what this moment means to you and what it signifies.

During the times of centering, open the journal and let it become your potter's wheel. The pages can quickly spin your life story before your eyes. You will begin to see a certain perspective shaping up from your past. Suddenly you will remember feelings and connotations that had eluded you. Definite shaping will already have started to happen.

Next, every one of us needs to practice meditation. In finding our center we also need to learn how to pull feelings and ideas deep down inside us. Once we get them beneath our mental and spiritual microscopes, we examine every side and dimension of our experience. We mentally chew up these bites of reality until they can be digested just as we do with food.

Often it takes considerable time just to clear our minds of distractions before the meditating can really begin. For this reason I keep a piece of paper close by. As distractions come up, I can jot them down for later action. Once I dispense with these interruptions, my mind can focus on the issues. Sometimes, just clearing my mind of the distractions restores balance and perspective.

Finally, centering demands solitude. It is not possible to become centered while careening through freeway traffic. Personally, I can't appropriate the Imago or develop my sense of God-given destiny while reading a book or listening to a speech or television program. While they may all help or hinder my quest, I finally have to be alone and quiet to let these new forces reshape my life. I am convinced that everyone needs a certain amount of time alone every day. In these quiet moments my life becomes stabilized. Only in such times of solitude can my mental and emotional needs get centered. Only in the quietness of reflection can I make the answers in this book become my personal possessions.

A CONCLUDING GRASP FOR SANITY

We have gone on a considerable journey together through these pages and chapters. We began searching for a way not to go crazy and have ended by learning how to stay sane. The sources for the loss of social identity and the confusion over personal identity have been discussed. Answers and new directions have been proposed. Ways of implementing the ideas have been presented.

The rest remains with you. I know there is no reason for you not to be able to live a sane, healthy, happy life.

You just need the confidence to make the right decisions and to do something about your intentions. Personal stability *is* within your grasp.

1. William Safire, "From Kooks to Flakes," in *The New York Times Magazine*, June 3, 1979, page 10.
2. *The Daily Oklahoman*, September 29, 1977.
3. *The Oklahoma Observer*, February 25, 1979, page 6.
4. C.S. Lewis, *Mere Christianity* (New York: The MacMillan Co., 1952).
5. Matthew chapters 5-7.
6. *The Random House Dictionary of the English Language*, Unabridged Edition (New York: Random House, 1970), page 15.